CARMEN

"There she is. There's our Carmencita."
Act One

GEORGES BIZET'S

CARMEN

AN ILLUSTRATED LIBRETTO

ORIGINAL FRENCH
BY H. MEILHAC AND L. HALÉVY

NEW ENGLISH TRANSLATION
BY SONYA FRIEDMAN

ILLUSTRATIONS BY RENÉ BULL

PARK LANE PRESS
New York • Avenel

This 1996 edition is published by Park Lane Press,
a division of Random House Value Publishing, Inc.,
40 Engelhard Avenue, Avenel, New Jersey 07001.

Park Lane Press and colophon are trademarks of
Random House Value Publishing, Inc.

Random House
New York • Toronto • London • Sydney • Auckland

Book design by Lisa Chovnick

Printed and bound in Singapore

Library of Congress Cataloging-in-Publication Data
Bizet, Georges, 1838–1875.
[Carmen. Libretto. English & French]
Georges Bizet's Carmen.
p. cm.
Includes original French libretto by Henri Meilhac and Ludovic Halévy, after
the novel by Prosper Mérimée, and English translation by Sonya Friedman.
ISBN 0–517–20002–3
1. Operas—Librettos. I. Meilhac, Henri, 1831–1897. II. Halévy, Ludovic,
1834–1908. III. Friedman, Sonya, 1932– . IV. Mérimée, Prosper, 1803–1870.
Carmen. V. Title.
ML50.B625C22   1996 <Case>
782.1'026'8—dc20   96–11775
                                                        CIP
                                                        M

8 7 6 5 4 3 2 1

CONTENTS

FOREWORD

GEORGES BIZET, BORN IN PARIS on October 25, 1838, was the son of professional musicians. A child prodigy who entered the Paris Conservatory at the age of nine, Bizet composed instrumental music in his teens and won the prestigious Grand Prix de Rome in 1857. That same year he was awarded a prize given by Offenbach for a one-act opera, *Dr. Miracle*. Following his return to Paris from Italy, Bizet wrote and produced three operas: *Les Pêcheurs de Perles*, The Pearlfishers (1863); *La Jolie Fille de Perth*, The Fair Maid of Perth (1867), and *Djamileh* (1872). These works, however, failed to bring him fame; nor was his incidental music for Daudet's *L'Arlesienne* the public and critical success it would yet become upon its revival in 1885.

Camille du Locle, director of the Opéra-Comique, is credited with suggesting to Bizet the composition of his next opera, *Carmen*. The story line originated in a widely successful novella by Prosper Merimée, who himself had expanded upon a dark tale of an Englishman's adventures with Spanish gypsies.

On March 3, 1875, the curtain at the Opéra-Comique rose on a grand opera that featured so many novelties that it brought new life to the genre itself. Not only did the text written by Henri Meilhac and Ludovic Halévy tell a story of ill-fated love and human imperfection, but it did so with a quality of realism usually absent from the form. In its first performance, *Carmen* contained spoken dialogue instead of the traditional musical recitatives. The score also kept pace with the passionate and violent feelings expressed by Carmen and Don José. The musical characterization of the corporal in his progressive decline from honest soldier to murderer is as vividly and audaciously rendered as Carmen's fiery spirit, her courage, and her fatalism.

vii

The production of the new opera was fraught with difficulties. The score Bizet had written was dense with ensembles the choruses were not accustomed to performing: they had to smoke, quarrel, and move about the stage in a totally new way. In fact, the chorus threatened to strike, and the orchestra complained that certain passages were unplayable.

The reception of both the public and the press was very critical. Bizet was accused of immorality, and obscenity; his sense of theater was qualified as poor, his taste as bad. The murder of the heroine on stage shocked an audience accustomed to happy endings. The press attacked the musical innovations Bizet had introduced—his use of flamenco rhythms, the harmonics and ensembles that were designed to illustrate and advance the drama. His use of recurring themes was denounced as imitative of Wagner.

Carmen was not the great success Bizet had hoped for, but neither was it a failure. There were thirty-five performances in the spring of 1875, and thirteen more the following season, many more than any of Bizet's other operas.

Bizet died three months after the opening of *Carmen*. It was only with its first revival eight years after the composer's death that *Carmen* became the beloved opera that it remains to this day. The realism and tragic strength that scandalized Bizet's contemporaries had a deep and lasting influence on composers who came after him and has moved audiences the world over ever since.

HÉLÈNE G. POTTER

New York
1996

COLOR ILLUSTRATIONS

THE STORY

ACT I

THE SETTING IS A SQUARE IN SEVILLE, at the beginning of the
nineteenth century. A company of dragoons posted there
relaxes outside the barracks. The officer on duty, Morales,
notices Micaela, a young peasant girl who is shyly making
inquiries about a corporal, Don José. She quickly withdraws
as Morales shows an interest in her. As Don José and the rest
of the relief guard arrive, they are mimicked by a crowd of
children. Just then, the women from the local cigarette factory
come out. Among them is Carmen, a gypsy girl of great beauty
and audacity, who sings to her admirers of the fickleness of love.
Noticing Don José's indifference, she attempts to entice him by
throwing him a flower. She disappears into the factory as
Micaela returns to give Don José news from his mother. After
Micaela departs, Don José reads his mother's letter; he vows to
honor his mother's wishes and marry Micaela. Meanwhile, a
fight has broken out in the factory, and the girls come out,
accusing Carmen of wounding one of the cigarette workers.
Carmen is arrested. Don José, assigned to guard her, agrees to
help her escape upon her promise of love. As the dragoons try
take her to prison, she breaks away.

ACT II

IN LILLAS PASTIA'S INN, where she has found refuge, Carmen
and her friends Frasquita and Mercedes praise the joys of
gypsy life. The toreador Escamillo, surrounded by admirers,
tells of his adventures in the bullring. He notices Carmen and
soon falls under her spell. The toreador and his party depart,

and Carmen and her companions are approached by Remendado and Dancairo, two smugglers who convince the women to join them on a smuggling expedition. Don José arrives, free from prison, where he had been disciplined by dragoon lieutenant Zuniga for letting the gypsy escape. Carmen dances for Don José to entice him to follow her into the mountains. Torn between his military obligations and his passion, Don José first refuses to follow her. However, when Zuniga enters the inn and orders him back to the barracks, Don José disobeys. A fight seems all but inevitable; but the gypsies disarm Zuniga, thereby forcing Don José to desert. Now on the run, Don José goes into hiding in the mountains with Carmen.

ACT III

THE PARTY OF GYPSIES, smugglers, and Don José pauses in a mountain pass. Carmen's infatuation with Don José is fading. The gypsy women read their fortunes from the cards. Carmen's cards speak only of death. Micaela appears, but hurriedly hides as Escamillo arrives, looking for Carmen. A confrontation ensues between the toreador and the corporal, knives come out, and Carmen barely manages to keep the two men apart. Escamillo leaves after inviting Carmen to the bullfights in Seville. As the smugglers are about to resume their march, Micaela is discovered. She convinces Don José to go with her to see his dying mother. Don José leaves, warning a defiant Carmen.

ACT IV

ON A FESTIVE SUNDAY IN SEVILLE, crowds gather for the bull-fight. A colorful procession makes its way to the arena. Escamillo appears with Carmen on his arm. As Escamillo goes off to earn his triumph, Carmen, despite being warned by her friends of danger, confronts Don José, now a broken man. He begs her to come back to him, but Carmen, arrogant and cruel, throws Don José's ring at his feet. As echoes of Escamillo's triumph reach them from the arena, Don José, crazed with jealousy, hurls himself at Carmen and stabs her to death.

THE CHARACTERS

CARMEN a gypsy girl who works at the
cigarette factory   Soprano

MICAELA a peasant girl   Soprano

MERCEDES ⎱
FRASQUITA ⎰ gypsy friends of Carmen   Mezzo-Soprano
                                                    Mezzo-Soprano

DON JOSÉ a corporal in the dragoons   Tenor

ESCAMILLO a toreador   Baritone

MORALES another corporal in the dragoons   Bass

ZUNIGA a lieutenant in the dragoons   Bass

EL REMENDADO ⎱
EL DANCAIRO ⎰ smugglers   Tenor
                                                    Baritone

INNKEEPER, GUIDE, DRAGOONS, CHILDREN,
FACTORY GIRLS, GYPSIES, SMUGGLERS

PLACE: In and near Seville   TIME: About 1820

SCENE ONE

A public square in Seville. On the right is the entrance to a tobacco factory. Beyond the factory door is a winding staircase leading to a bridge that stretches from one side of the stage to the other. At the left is a guardhouse. As the curtain rises, Morales and a group of soldiers (the dragoons of Alcalá) are in front of the guardhouse, smoking and watching people actively passing in all directions.

SOLDIERS
Everyone passes by this square;
people coming, going,
    here and there.
All sorts of odd characters!

1

MORALES

We soldiers on guard are just killing time;
we smoke, we gossip, we stare
    at all the strollers everywhere.
Everyone passes by this square;
people coming, going,
    here and there.
All sorts of odd characters!

(Micaela enters; she seems hesitant, ill at ease. She looks at the soldiers, starts toward them, then draws back.)

MORALES

Look at that pretty young girl.
It seems she wants to talk to us.
Look! Look!
Oh, but she's hesitating, she's turning away.

SOLDIERS

It's our duty to help her out!

MORALES *(to Micaela)*

Are you looking for someone, my beauty?

MICAELA

I'm looking for a corporal in the guard.

MORALES

Well, here I am!

MICAELA

My córporal's name is Don José.
Do you know him?

MORALES

Don José? We all know him.

MICAELA

Really? Please tell me, is he here?

MORALES
He's not a corporal in our company.

MICAELA *(disappointed)*
Then he isn't here.

MORALES
No, my charming girl, he isn't here.
But very shortly, he'll appear.
And finding him won't be hard,
when his company arrives
for the changing of the guard.

SOLDIERS AND MORALES
Finding him won't be hard,
when his company arrives
for the changing of the guard.

MORALES
While you're waiting for him, my little beauty,
wouldn't you like to step inside
our guardhouse for a moment?

MICAELA
With you?

SOLDIERS
With us!

MICAELA
With you?

SOLDIERS
With us!

MICAELA
Oh, no, no.
Thanks all the same, gentlemen.

MORALES

No need to worry, sweetheart.
I promise you we'll treat
a sweet little lady like you
with all the respect you deserve.

MICAELA

I don't doubt it.
All the same, I'll come back later.
It's better that way.
(slyly)
And finding him won't be hard,
when his company arrives
for the changing of the guard.
And finding him won't be hard
when his company arrives
for the changing of the guard.

SOLDIERS AND MORALES *(surrounding Micaela)*
You should stay, because the new guard
is just about to relieve the old one.

IN UNISON

MORALES

Do stay!

MICAELA

Oh, no. Oh, no.
Good-bye for now, gentlemen.

(She runs off.)

MORALES

Our little bird has flown.
Well, let's find some other amusement.
Let's go back to killing time,
watching the people passing by.

SOLDIERS
Everyone passes by this square;
people coming, going,
        here and there.
All sorts of odd characters!

SCENE TWO

*A distant bugle call from off-scene is answered by a trumpet in the
orchestra. An officer comes out of the guardhouse. The soldiers
take up their lances and form ranks. The passersby stop to watch
the parade. Street urchins come running in from all sides. The
relief guard appears: first, two fifes and a bugler; then Zuniga,
Don José, and the soldiers. The street urchins march in step,
following the dragoons.*

CHORUS OF STREET URCHINS
Here we are!
We've come with the changing of the guard.
Blow the bugle! Louder, louder!
Tara-ta-ta, tara-ta-ta!

Heads held high, we march
like little soldiers.
We're never out of step.
Left, right, in perfect time.

Shoulders back! Chests out!
Our arms swinging straight,
close to our sides.

Here we are!
We've come with the changing of the guard!
Sound the bugle! Louder! Louder!
Tara-ta-ta, tara-ta-ta.

(The relief guard halts, facing the guard on duty. As the children continue singing, the officers salute each other with their swords, then stand talking in low voices as the sentry is changed.)

MORALES *(to Don José)*
A charming girl was here asking for you.
Blue skirt, and long, braided hair.

DON JOSÉ
That must be Micaela.

(The old guard passes before the new guard. The urchins line up behind the old guard, and again march behind the bugler and fifes, just as they had marched behind the relief guard.)

CHORUS OF URCHINS *(reprise)*
Off goes the old guard, back to their barracks.
Sound the trumpets. Louder! Louder!
Tara-ta-ta, tara-ta-ta!

Heads held high, we march
like little soldiers.
We're never out of step.
Left, right, in perfect time.

(The soldiers gradually exit; the urchins disappear. The onlookers drift away in the background. Zuniga authorizes his soldiers to break ranks, and the dragoons disperse, some entering the guard-house. Zuniga joins Don José.)

ZUNIGA
Isn't that big building over there
where the cigarette girls work?

DON JOSÉ
It is, sir. And you've never seen girls
of such easy virtue!

ZUNIGA

Well, are they pretty at least?

DON JOSÉ

Sir, I really wouldn't know.
I don't pay attention to such things.

ZUNIGA

I know very well what you pay attention to,
    my friend.
A charming young girl by the name of Micaela.
Blue skirt, and long, braided hair.
What do you say to that?

DON JOSÉ

I say, it's true.
I say, I love her!
As for the factory girls over there,
you can judge for yourself
whether they're beautiful or not.
Here they come.

(The factory bell is heard. The square fills with passersby and with young men who have come to meet the cigarette-factory girls. The soldiers come out of the guardhouse. Don José is seated, repairing a small chain, indifferent to what is going on around him.)

YOUNG MEN

The bell has rung,
and we're eagerly waiting
for the factory girls to come out.
We'll follow them around,
those dark-haired cigarette girls,
as we murmur sweet proposals of love,
proposals of love, proposals of love.

(The cigarette-factory girls appear, smoking cigarettes. Slowly, they drift downstage.)

SOLDIERS

Look at them! Such brazen glances,
so flirtatious!
And they're all smoking,
holding their cigarettes
between their teeth.

CIGARETTE GIRLS

We watch the floating smoke rings
rise up into the sky.
Up they waft,
in a fragrant cloud.
The smoke goes to your head,
softly, sweetly.
And your heart feels like it's on holiday!

The sweet talk of lovers?
Up in smoke!
Their raptures and their promises?
Up in smoke!
We watch the floating smoke rings
rise up into the sky.

YOUNG MEN

Don't be so cruel.
Listen to us, you beauties.
We adore you,
we idolize you!

CIGARETTE GIRLS

The sweet talk of lovers?
Their raptures and their promises?
Up in smoke!
We watch the floating smoke rings
rise up into the sky.
All smoke . . . !

YOUNG MEN

It's you we love!
Listen to us, you beauties.

"Hey, soldier. What are you doing there?"
Act One

SOLDIERS

But where's our favorite?
Our Carmencita?

(Carmen enters. She holds a flower in her mouth, and wears a corsage at her waist.)

YOUNG MEN

There she is!

SOLDIERS

There she is!

YOUNG MEN AND CIGARETTE GIRLS

There she is.
There's our Carmencita.

YOUNG MEN *(surrounding Carmen)*

Carmen, we'll follow you to the ends of the earth.
Carmen, have a heart. At least give us an answer.
When will you give us your love? Name the day!

CARMEN *(after a swift glance at Don José)*
When will I love you?
Really, I can't say.
Maybe never. Maybe tomorrow.
But certainly not today.

Love is a wild bird
that no one can tame.
It's useless to chase it,
if it won't play the game.
Threats, pleas, it's all the same.
One man smooth-talks,
the other doesn't say a word.
And the one that says nothing
is the one my heart has heard!
That's love, that's love!
        (chorus)
Love is a gypsy child
who doesn't know what rules are about.
If you don't love me, I may love you.
And if I love you, watch out!

The bird you caught by surprise
beats its wings, and off it flies.
Love ignores you; you wait and mope.
Then there it is—when you give up hope.
Love's all around you. Quick, quick!
You have no man, or you have your pick.
Think you've found love?
It turns you down cold.
Think you've escaped it?
It has you in its hold.
That's love, that's love!
        (chorus)
Love is a gypsy child
who doesn't know what rules are about.
If you don't love me, I may love you.
And if I love you, watch out!

Young Men

Carmen, we'll follow you to the ends of the earth.
Carmen, have a heart. At least give us an answer.

(After a pause, the young men surround Carmen, who looks at them one by one. Then she breaks through their circle and walks straight to Don José, who is still working on his chain.)

Carmen

Hey, soldier, what are you doing there?

Don José

Trying to fix this chain.

Carmen

Your chain? Why not try for my heart?

(Carmen throws a flower at Don José, who jumps to his feet. The crowd laughs. The factory bell rings again. Carmen runs into the factory. The cigarette girls crowd around Don José.)

Cigarette Girls

Love is a gypsy child
who doesn't know what rules are about.
If you don't love me, I may love you.
And if I love you, watch out!

(The cigarette girls go back into the factory. The young men and the onlookers exit. The soldiers go into the guardhouse. Don José is left alone. He picks up the flower.)

Don José

What a look she gave me! What nerve!
This flower that she threw
struck me like a bullet.
What a strong scent it has.
That woman . . .
she's a sorceress if there ever was one.

(Micaela enters.)

MICAELA

José!

DON JOSÉ

Micaela!

MICAELA

Yes, here I am.

DON JOSÉ

How wonderful!

MICAELA

Your mother sent me to you.

DON JOSÉ

Tell me all about my mother.

MICAELA

She sent me as her trusted
    messenger
to bring you this letter.

DON JOSÉ

A letter!

MICAELA

And a little money
to add to your pay.
(She gives him a small purse.)
And also . . .

DON JOSÉ

Something else?

MICAELA

Something else that . . .
really, I don't dare.
Something else worth more than
    money
to any loving son.

DON JOSÉ
What is it? Tell me.

MICAELA
All right, I'll tell you.
I promised to give you something
that she gave to me.
Your mother and I were just leaving church,
when she embraced me.
"Go to the city," she told me.
"It's not very far. And once you're in Seville,
find my son, my Don José, my dear child.
And tell him that his mother
dreams of him night and day.
That she misses him, that she longs for him,
that she forgives him for everything in the past,
and that she waits for him.
All this, my dear,
tell him for me.
And this kiss that I give you . . .
give him for me."

DON JOSÉ *(moved)*
A kiss from my mother!

MICAELA
A kiss for her son.
Don José, I'll kiss you for her
just as I promised.

(Micaela stands on tiptoe, and gives Don José a maternal, affectionate kiss. Don José is extremely moved. He looks into Micaela's eyes, without speaking for a moment.)

DON JOSÉ
I can see my mother's face.
Yes, I can see my own village again.
Oh, memories from long ago,
Sweet memories of home.
Sweet memories of home,
What precious memories!

Oh, memories, precious memories.
They fill my heart with strength and courage

MICAELA

He can see his mother's face.
He can see his own village again.
Oh, what memories!
Sweet memories of home.
They fill his heart with strength and courage.
What precious memories!

DON JOSÉ *(musing to himself)*

Who knows what demon might have
    overpowered me?
From far away, my mother is protecting me
with the kiss she sent.
She's saving her son from the danger he's facing.

MICAELA

What demon? What danger? I don't understand.
What do you mean?

DON JOSÉ

Nothing, nothing.
Let's talk about you, my sweet messenger.
Are you going back to our village?

MICAELA

Yes, this evening. Tomorrow, I'll see your mother.

DON JOSÉ

You'll see her! Good. Then tell her
that her son loves her and respects her.
And that he's sorry for any wrong he's done
    in the past.
He only wants his mother to be proud of him.
Tell her all that, dear girl, tell her for me.
And this kiss I give you,
give her for me.

(He kisses her.)

MICAELA
Yes, I promise. I'll give her your message,
and, Don José, I'll kiss her for you as I promised.

DON JOSÉ
I can see my mother's face.
Yes, I can see my own village again.
Oh, memories from long ago,
sweet memories of home.
Sweet memories of home,
What precious memories!
Oh, memories, precious memories.
They fill my heart with strength and courage.

MICAELA
He can see his mother's face.
He can see his own village again.
Oh, what memories!
Sweet memories of home.
They fill his heart with strength and courage.
What precious memories!

DON JOSÉ
Now sit down while I read
what she has to say.

MICAELA
No, you go on and read.
I'll come back later.

DON JOSÉ
Why are you leaving?

MICAELA
It's better that way.
I prefer it.
Read it. Then I'll come back.

DON JOSÉ
You're sure you'll come back?

MICAELA

I'm sure.

(She exits. Don José reads the letter.)

DON JOSÉ

Don't you worry, Mother. Your son will obey you.
He'll do as you say. I love Micaela,
and I'll make her my wife.

As for your flower, you sorceress . . . !

(Screams are heard from the factory. Zuniga enters, followed by soldiers.)

ZUNIGA

What's going on in there?

(The factory girls enter in an uproar.)

FIRST GROUP OF GIRLS

Help! Didn't you hear us?

SECOND GROUP OF GIRLS

Help us, soldiers!

FIRST GROUP

It was Carmencita!

SECOND GROUP

No, no, it wasn't her!

FIRST GROUP

It was her!

SECOND GROUP

Not at all!

FIRST GROUP

She did it! It was her!
She struck the first blow!

ALL THE GIRLS *(surrounding Zuniga)*
Don't listen to them!
Don't listen to them!
Listen to us! To us!

SECOND GROUP *(drawing him aside)*
Manuelita kept repeating
in her loud, shrill voice
that she was definitely going to buy
a donkey that she liked.

FIRST GROUP *(pulling Zuniga to their side)*
Then Carmen answered,
in her usual sarcastic way,
"A donkey? What for?
You should be riding a broom!"

SECOND GROUP
Then Manuelita snapped back
at her not-so-favorite friend:
"It's because *you're* an ass
that you talk as you do!"

FIRST GROUP
"I can see it now," said Carmen.
"You'll be putting on airs,
and hiring two servants to follow behind,
to shoo the flies off of you!"

BOTH GROUPS
Then the squabbling pair
grabbed each other by the hair.

ZUNIGA
To the devil with these women and their quarrels!
Don José, take two men with you.
Go inside and see who started this argument.

*(Don José takes two soldiers with him and they exit into the factory.
Meanwhile, the girls argue among themselves.)*

FIRST GROUP
It was Carmencita!

SECOND GROUP
No, no, she didn't start it!

ZUNIGA
Stop!
Get these women away from me!

BOTH GROUPS
Sir, don't listen to them! Listen to us!

(The soldiers push the girls back, and clear the square. Carmen appears at the factory door, led by Don José, and followed by two dragoons.)

DON JOSÉ
Sir, there was a quarrel.
First, some insults,
then blows.
A woman was wounded.

ZUNIGA
By whom?

DON JOSÉ *(indicating Carmen)*
This one here.

ZUNIGA
You heard that. What do you have to say?

CARMEN
Tra-la-la-la-la,
Cut me, burn me,
I'm not talking.
Tra-la-la-la-la,
Nothing scares me. Not fire,
swords, not heaven itself!

ZUNIGA

I didn't ask you for songs.
When someone asks you a question,
give him an answer!

CARMEN

Tra-la-la-la-la,
I'm keeping my secret to myself.
Tra-la-la-la-la,
I love a certain someone,
and I'll love him till I die.

ZUNIGA

The same old tune.
Well, you can sing your song to the four walls . . .
in jail!

FACTORY GIRLS

In jail! In jail!

*(Carmen tries to attack the women. The soldiers drive the women
out of the square.)*

ZUNIGA

Damn you!
You're pretty free with your hands.

CARMEN

Tra-la-la-la-la . . .

ZUNIGA

It's a pity, a great pity.
Because she's really a beauty.
But she needs to be tamed.
You'd better tie up those pretty hands of hers.

(Zuniga exits into the guardhouse with the other soldiers.)

CARMEN

Where are you taking me?

DON JOSÉ

To jail. There's nothing I can do about it now.

CARMEN

There's really nothing you can do?

DON JOSÉ

No, nothing. I'm obeying orders.

CARMEN

Know what? In spite of your orders,
you'll do what I ask you to.
Know why? Because you love me.

DON JOSÉ

Me? Love you?

CARMEN

Yes, José. That flower I gave you . . .
you know, that flower has a spell on it.
You can throw it away now.
The spell's already at work.

DON JOSÉ
Don't you talk to me anymore! You understand?
Don't talk anymore. I forbid you to.

CARMEN
Very well, Officer, sir.
If you forbid me to talk, I won't talk.

Outside the walls of Seville,
at the inn of Lillas Pastia,
I'll dance the seguidilla
and drink Manzanilla.
I'll go to my friend Lillas Pastia.
But I'll be bored all alone.
You need two for pleasure.
So to keep myself company,
I'll take along my lover.

What lover?
He's gone to the devil.
I just threw him out yesterday.
But my broken heart mends fast.
My heart is free as the air.

I've got dozens of men,
but they don't appeal to me.
Here it is the weekend.
Who wants my love?
I'll give him my love!

Who wants my heart?
It's yours for the taking.
I've got no time to waste,
because with my new lover . . .

. . . outside the walls of Seville,
at the inn of Lillas Pastia,
I'll dance the seguidilla
and drink Manzanilla.
Yes, I'll go to my friend Lillas Pastia.

DON JOSÉ

Quiet! I told you not to talk to me.

CARMEN

I'm not talking to you. I'm singing to myself.
I'm singing to myself, and I'm thinking.
It's not against the law to think.
I'm thinking of a certain soldier.
I'm thinking of a certain soldier who loves me.
And as for me . . .
yes, as for me, I could fall in love with him!

DON JOSÉ

Carmen!

CARMEN

My soldier isn't a captain.
He isn't even a lieutenant.
He's just a corporal.
But that's enough for a gypsy like me.
And I'd be satisfied with him.

DON JOSÉ

Carmen, I'm like a man gone mad!
If I agree, if I give in to you,
will you keep your promise?
Oh, if I love you, Carmen . . .
Carmen, will you love me?

CARMEN

Yes.

DON JOSÉ

At Lillas Pastia's . . .

CARMEN

We'll dance the seguidilla . . .

DON JOSÉ

You promise? Carmen!

CARMEN
. . . and drink Manzanilla.

DON JOSÉ
You promise?

(He unties the rope around her wrists.)

CARMEN *(triumphantly)*
Ah! Outside the walls of Seville,
at the inn of Lillas Pastia,
I'll dance the seguidilla
and drink Manzanilla.
Tra-la-la-la-la-la.

(Zuniga comes out of the guardhouse with two soldiers.)

ZUNIGA
Here's the arrest warrant. Take her away.
And keep an eye on her.

CARMEN *(aside to Don José)*
As we leave, I'll give you a push.
A real hard push.
Fall down, and leave the rest to me.

CARMEN *(laughing at Zuniga)*
Love is a gypsy child
who doesn't know what rules are about.
If you don't love me, I may love you.
And if I love you, watch out!
If you don't love me, if you don't love me,
I may love you.
But if I love you, if I love you,
Watch out!

(Carmen marches off with Don José and the soldiers. At the bridge, she pushes Don José. He falls and she escapes, laughing loudly.)

"As we leave, I'll give you a push."
Act One

ACT TWO

SCENE ONE

*Lillas Pastia's inn. When the curtain rises, Carmen, Frasquita, and
Mercedes are at a table with Morales, Lieutenant Zuniga, and
other officers. They have just finished eating and the tables are in
disarray. Two gypsy men play guitars in the corner of the tavern,
and two gypsy women dance center stage.*

CARMEN
A metallic rhythm vibrates in the air.
And the gypsies rise to this strange music.
The Basque tambourines hold sway.
And under stubborn fingers,
the frenzied guitars carry
    out their familiar song.
Tra la la la la la.

Copper and silver rings
glitter on the dancers'
    dark skins.
Orange and red striped
    skirts
flutter in the breeze.
The dance is wedded to the song.
At first, it's hesitant.
But soon it grows lively.
And then it rises, rises, rises!
Tra la la la la la.

The gypsies drive on,
their music, a blinding roar.

And the pulsating rhythm
holds the gypsy women spellbound.
At the beat of the music,
wild, frenzied, feverish,
they become intoxicated,
and let themselves be swept away
on a whirlwind of music!
Tra la la la la la.

(The dance becomes fast, frenzied. Carmen joins in, then at the last notes, collapses on a table.)

FRASQUITA
Friends, Pastia just told me . . .

ZUNIGA
What does Lillas Pastia want now?

FRASQUITA
He says the chief of police wants him
to close up the inn now.

ZUNIGA
All right, we're leaving. You girls come with us.

FRASQUITA
We can't. We have to stay.

ZUNIGA
And you, Carmen, you're not coming?
Listen. Just two words. You're angry with me.

CARMEN
Angry with you? Why?

ZUNIGA
Because of that soldier who went to jail for you.

CARMEN
What happened to that poor boy?

ZUNIGA

He was just released today.

CARMEN

So he's free! That's fine.
Good night, soldier lover-boys.

FRASQUITA, MERCEDES, CARMEN

Good night, soldier lover-boys!

CHORUS *(off stage)*

Hoorah, hoorah for the torero!
Hoorah for Escamillo! Hoorah, hoorah!

ZUNIGA

There's a torchlight parade
for the winner of the bullfights at Granada.
(calling out the window)
        Would you have a drink with us, my friend?
        To toast your past successes, and your future ones!

(The torero Escamillo and his entourage enter.)

ZUNIGA AND CHORUS

Hoorah! Hoorah for the torero!

CARMEN, FRASQUITA, MERCEDES

Hoorah! Hoorah for the torero!
Long live Escamillo! Hoorah for Escamillo!
Hoorah, hoorah!

ESCAMILLO

I toast you as well, Señors.
For soldiers, like bullfighters,
truly understand the joy of battle.

The arena is full.
It's a holiday.
The area is packed from top to bottom.
The fans go wild.
The fans are in an uproar.

"Dream of the love that's waiting for you, Toreador!"
Act Two

They're shouting, they're stamping,
they're clapping furiously.
It's a celebration of courage,
a celebration for men with heart!

Ready! On guard!
Ready! On guard!

Toreador, on guard! Toreador, toreador!
And as you fight, yes,
dream of the dark eyes watching you.
And of the love that's waiting for you, Toreador.
The love, the love that's waiting for you!

FRASQUITA AND MERCEDES

Toreador, on guard! Toreador, toreador!
And as you fight, yes,
dream of those dark eyes watching you.
And of the love that's waiting for you, Toreador.
The love, the love that's waiting for you.

ESCAMILLO

Suddenly, it's silent. Deadly silent.
What has happened?
No more shouting, the moment has come!
No more shouting, the moment is here!
The bull leaps into the ring.
He bounds out from behind the fence.
He enters, he charges, he strikes!
A horse falls, dragging down a picador.
"Hurrah for the bull!" screams the crowd.
The bull turns again, charges again,
strikes again!

He shakes the banderillas in his back.
He runs, mad with pain.
The ring is full of blood.
Everyone escapes, runs behind the barriers.
And it's your turn now.
Ready! On guard!
Toreador, on guard!

ENTIRE GROUP
Toreador, on guard!

(Everyone takes a drink, then clasps hands with the torero. The officers get ready to leave. Escamillo draws near to Carmen.)

ESCAMILLO
One word, my beauty.
What's your name?
The next time I face death,
I want to say your name.

CARMEN
Carmen. Carmencita.
Either one, it's all the same to me.

ESCAMILLO
What if someone told you he loves you?

CARMEN
I'd advise him not to love me.

ESCAMILLO
That's not an inviting answer.
I'll just have to wait, and hope.

CARMEN
It's not against the law to wait.
And it's sweet to hope.

ZUNIGA
Since you won't come with me, Carmen,
    I'll be back.

CARMEN
You'll be making a big mistake.

ZUNIGA
I'll take my chances.

ESCAMILLO *(spoken)*
My friends, I thank all of you.

(Escamillo and his friends exit, along with Zuniga and the soldiers. The smugglers El Dancairo and El Remendado enter.)

SCENE TWO

FRASQUITA
Quick, tell me the news.

EL DANCAIRO
The news isn't bad.
We can make quite a killing.
But we'll need your help.

FRASQUITA, MERCEDES, CARMEN
Our help?

EL DANCAIRO
Yes, we're depending on you.
We have a job in mind.

MERCEDES, THEN FRASQUITA
A good one? Tell us.

EL DANCAIRO
It's a great scheme, my dear.
But we need you ladies!

EL REMENDADO
Yes, we need you ladies.

CARMEN
You need us?

EL REMENDADO

Yes, you!

FRASQUITA

Us?

EL REMENDADO

You!

MERCEDES

Us?

EL REMENDADO

You!

CARMEN, FRASQUITA, MERCEDES

You need us? Really!
You really do need us?

EL REMENDADO AND EL DANCAIRO

Because we admit, most humbly
and with the greatest respect,
that when it comes to cheating,
lying, and stealing,
it's always best—we swear it!—
to have the ladies along.
Without you beauties, everything goes wrong!

CARMEN, FRASQUITA, MERCEDES

Well! Without us, everything goes wrong.
Everything! Right?

EL REMENDADO AND EL DANCAIRO

Don't you agree with us?

CARMEN, FRASQUITA, MERCEDES

It seems to me, we do agree.
When it comes to cheating,
lying and stealing,
it's always best—we swear it!—

to have us ladies along.
Without us beauties, everything goes wrong.

EL DANCAIRO
We all agree, then. So you're ready to leave?

FRASQUITA
Whenever you say.

MERCEDES
Whenever you say.

EL DANCAIRO
Then I say, right away.

CARMEN
Oh, wait, not so fast, not so fast.
If you want to leave, go ahead.
But count me out. I'm staying here.
I'm staying right here.

EL REMENDADO
Carmen, sweetheart, you've got to come.
You wouldn't have the heart to leave us in the
     lurch!

FRASQUITA AND MERCEDES
Oh, Carmen dear, of course you'll come.

CARMEN
I'm not leaving, I'm not, I'm not, I'm not.

EL DANCAIRO
But at least give us a reason, Carmen.
Tell us why.

**MERCEDES, FRASQUITA,
EL REMENDADO, EL DANCAIRO**
Give us a reason, a reason!

CARMEN
Certainly, I'll explain it to you.

**EL DANCAIRO, THEN EL REMENDADO,
MERCEDES, AND FRASQUITA**
Go on, go on!

CARMEN
The reason is that right now . . .

**EL DANCAIRO, THEN EL REMENDADO,
MERCEDES, AND FRASQUITA**
Right now what?

CARMEN
I'm in love!

EL REMENDADO AND EL DANCAIRO
What did she say?

FRASQUITA AND MERCEDES
She says she's in love. In love!

EL REMENDADO AND EL DANCAIRO
In love! In love!

CARMEN
Yes, I'm in love.

EL DANCAIRO
Come on, Carmen, be serious.

CARMEN
I'm wildly, madly in love.

EL REMENDADO AND EL DANCAIRO *(ironically)*
We're really astonished.
But it isn't the first time.
My little pet, you've always managed
to mix love and business before.
You've always mixed love and business very well!

CARMEN

My friends, I'd be delighted to leave with you
    tonight.
But this time, please don't be disappointed,
love has to come before duty.

EL DANCAIRO

This isn't your final word?

CARMEN

Absolutely.

EL REMENDADO

You've just got to change your mind.

QUARTET

You've got to come with us, Carmen, you've got to.
It's urgent. We need you because . . .

CARMEN

Well, I agree I'd be very useful.

QUARTET

Because when it comes to thieving,
lying and cheating,
it's always best—we swear it!—
to have the women along.
Without those beauties, everything goes wrong.

EL DANCAIRO

Well, who are you waiting for?

CARMEN

Nobody important. A soldier who did me a favor
a while ago, and landed in jail because of me.

EL REMENDADO

A delicate situation.

EL DANCAIRO

Your soldier may have changed his mind in jail.
Are you really sure he'll come here?

(From off stage, we hear Don José approaching, singing.)

DON JOSÉ *(off stage)*

"Halt! Who goes there?"
—"A dragoon of Alcalá!"

CARMEN

Listen!

DON JOSÉ *(off stage)*

"Where are you going,
dragoon of Alcalá?"

CARMEN

There he is!

DON JOSÉ *(off stage)*

"I'm going to make my enemy
bite the dust.
I'll meet him and defeat him."
—"If that's so,
you may pass, my friend.
An affair of honor,
an affair of the heart,
that means all the world
To us dragoons of Alcalá!"

(Through the partly opened shutters, Frasquita, Mercedes, El Dancairo, and El Remendado look at Don José.)

FRASQUITA

He's a handsome dragoon.

MERCEDES

A very handsome dragoon!

EL DANCAIRO
He'd be a good man to have on our side.

EL REMENDADO
Tell him to come along with us.

CARMEN
He'd refuse.

EL DANCAIRO
Well, at least give it a try.

CARMEN
All right, I'll try.

DON JOSÉ *(coming nearer)*
"Halt! Who goes there?"
    —"A dragoon of Alcalá!"
"Where are you going,
dragoon of Alcalá?"
        —"Faithful and true,
    I go where I'm called.
    I go where my fair love beckons to me."

"If that's so,
 you may pass, my friend.
 An affair of honor,
 an affair of the heart,
 that means all the world
 to us dragoons of Alcalá!"

(Everyone except Carmen exits, just before Don José enters.)

S C E N E T H R E E

CARMEN

Finally! You're here!

DON JOSÉ

Carmen!

CARMEN

So you got out of prison?

DON JOSÉ

I was there for two months.

CARMEN

Do you regret it?

DON JOSÉ

Not at all. I'd have stayed there longer,
if it would have helped you.

CARMEN

Then you love me?

DON JOSÉ

I adore you!

"Then you love me?"
Act Two

CARMEN

Your officers were just here.
They had us dance for them.

DON JOSÉ

What? You, too?

CARMEN

Are you jealous, by any chance?

DON JOSÉ

Well, yes. I am jealous.

CARMEN

Calm down, my friend, calm down.
I'm going to dance in your honor.
And you'll see, Señor,
how well I accompany my own dance.

Sit right there, Don José.

(Carmen makes Don José sit down.)

CARMEN

I'm beginning!

(Carmen dances, accompanying herself on the castanets. After a moment, a military bugle is heard off stage. Don José rises, gesturing to Carmen to stop.)

DON JOSÉ

Wait a minute, Carmen.
Stop just for a moment.

CARMEN *(surprised)*
And why, may I ask?

DON JOSÉ

I thought I just heard . . .
Yes, those are our bugles sounding retreat.
Don't you hear them?

CARMEN

Wonderful, wonderful!
Now I'll have some accompaniment.
It's depressing to dance without any instruments.
But now we have this wonderful music
out of the blue!

(Carmen starts to dance again, with her castanets. Don José stops her.)

DON JOSÉ

You don't understand, Carmen.
It's the retreat.
I have to go back to the barracks.

CARMEN *(stupified)*

To the barracks? For retreat?
Oh, I've been an idiot!
A real idiot!
Here I am doing my best—my very best—
to amuse the gentleman.
I sing, I dance, I'm almost convinced,
God help me, that I'm falling in love with him!
Ta-ra-ta-ta.
Then the bugle sounds.
Ta-ra-ta-ta.
And off he goes!
Get out, sonny-boy!
Here, take your belt and your sword
    and your helmet.
And get out, my boy, go on!
Go back to your barracks!

DON JOSÉ

Carmen, it's not fair of you to taunt me.
It's painful for me to leave you.
Never, never before has any other woman
so troubled my heart.

"I'm going to dance in your honor."
Act Two

Carmen

CARMEN

Ta-ra-ta-ta.
My God, it's the retreat!
Ta-ra-ta-ta.
He's going to be late!
Oh, my God, my God, it's the retreat!
He'll be late!
So he loses his head,
and he runs off.
So much for his great love!

DON JOSÉ

Then you don't believe
    I love you?

CARMEN

No.

DON JOSÉ

Then listen to me!

CARMEN

I don't want to hear any more.

DON JOSÉ

Listen to me!

CARMEN

Go on, don't keep them waiting.

DON JOSÉ

You're going to hear me out!

CARMEN

You're keeping them all waiting.

DON JOSÉ

Carmen, you'll listen to me
whether you like it or not!

(From his vest, Don José draws out the flower Carmen had thrown at him. He shows it to Carmen.)

DON JOSÉ

Here's the flower you tossed at me.
I kept it with me in prison.
This flower is now faded and dry.
Yet it has still kept its sweet fragrance.
For hours on end, I pressed it
against my closed eyes.
I was drunk with its scent.
And all night long, I saw only you.
I began to curse you,
to hate you, and to ask myself
why fate had brought you
into my life.

Then I blamed myself.
And I felt, deep inside me,
only one desire.
Only one desire.
Only one hope.
To see you again, Carmen!
For you had only to appear,
and to cast one glance at me,
and I was completely yours!

Oh, my dearest Carmen.
Do whatever you want with me.
Carmen, I love you!

CARMEN

No, you don't love me.

DON JOSÉ

What are you saying?

CARMEN

No, you don't love me. No!
Because if you loved me,
you'd follow me out there, out there.

DON JOSÉ

Carmen!

CARMEN

Yes! Out there, out there, in the mountains.
Out there, out there, you'd come away with me.
You'd carry me away on your horse,
and like a true hero,
you'd ride into the hills.
Out there, out there, in the mountains.

DON JOSÉ

Carmen!

CARMEN

Out there, out there, in the mountains.
Out there, out there, you'd come away with me,
you'd follow me anywhere.
If you loved me!

You'd answer to no one.
There'd be no officers to obey.
No retreat telling you
it's time to leave your lover!
The open sky, life on the road . . .
the whole world as your country.
The law? Your own desires!
And above all, the intoxication
of freedom. Freedom!

DON JOSÉ

My God!

CARMEN

Out there, out there, in the mountains . . .

DON JOSÉ

Carmen!

CARMEN

Out there, out there, if you loved me . . .

DON JOSÉ

Be quiet!

CARMEN

Out there, you'd come away with me.
You'd carry me away on your horse.

DON JOSÉ

Carmen, for pity's sake, be quiet!
Be quiet! My God!

CARMEN

You'd carry me away on your horse,
and like a true hero,
you'd ride into the hills.
Out there, out there, in the mountains.
Yes, you'd carry me away,
if you loved me.

DON JOSÉ

No, Carmen, no!
Have pity on me, Carmen, have pity!
Oh, my God, be quiet!

CARMEN

Yes, you would do it.
Out there, out there, you'd carry me away,
carry me away.
If you loved me, you'd carry me away.
Out there, out there,
you'd go with me.

DON JOSÉ

Be quiet! Be quiet!

No! I won't listen to you anymore!
Abandon the army? Desert?
That's dishonorable! Shameful!
I won't do it!

CARMEN

Then get out!

DON JOSÉ

Carmen, I beg you!

CARMEN

No! I don't love you anymore.
Leave! I hate you! Good-bye.
Good-bye forever!

DON JOSÉ

Then so be it . . . good-bye forever.

CARMEN

Get out!

DON JOSÉ

Carmen, good-bye. Good-bye forever.

CARMEN

Good-bye.

(Don José runs toward the door. As he is about to open it, there is a knock from outside. Don José stops. There is a pause, then another knock.)

SCENE FOUR

ZUNIGA *(calling from outside)*
Carmen! Are you there?

DON JOSÉ

Who's knocking? Who's there?

CARMEN

Quiet! Don't talk!

(Zuniga forces the door, and enters.)

ZUNIGA
So I have to let myself in!

(He sees Don José, then turns to Carmen.)

Oh, too bad, too bad, my beauty.
You didn't make a good choice.
Why stoop to taking a soldier
when you could have an officer?

ZUNIGA *(to Don José)*
Now leave. Right now.

DON JOSÉ
No!

ZUNIGA
Go on. You're leaving!

DON JOSÉ
I'm not leaving.

ZUNIGA *(pushing Don José)*
Idiot!

DON JOSÉ *(drawing his sword)*
Damn you! We'll fight to the death!

CARMEN *(throwing herself between them)*
You jealous fool! Help! Help!

(El Dancairo, El Remendado, Mercedes, Frasquita, and the gypsies appear from all sides. At a gesture from Carmen, the men disarm Zuniga.)

CARMEN *(to Zuniga, mocking him)*
Well, my handsome officer,
love played a dirty trick on you.

You came at a bad time.
A very bad time. Too bad!
Now we'll have to keep you with us
for at least an hour.

EL REMENDADO AND EL DANCAIRO *(pistols in hand)*
We're going to leave the premises
if you don't mind.
Will you kindly join us?

CARMEN
For a little promenade?

GYPSY MEN
What's your answer, my friend?
Do you agree?

ZUNIGA *(accepting the situation)*
Certainly, now that I follow your reasoning.
You're very convincing.
But watch out . . . later on!

EL DANCAIRO
War is war.
Meanwhile, my good officer,
do go out ahead of us, if you please.

EL REMENDADO AND GYPSY MEN
Do go out ahead of us, if you please.

CARMEN *(to Don José)*
Are you one of us now?

DON JOSÉ
I have no choice!

CARMEN
That's not very gallant of you.
But never mind, you'll change.
You'll see how exciting
life on the road can be.

The whole world as your country.
The law? Your own desires!
And above all, the intoxication
of freedom. Freedom!

DON JOSÉ AND ENTIRE GROUP
The open skies! Life on the road.
The whole world as your country.
And the law? Your own desires.
And above all, the intoxication of freedom.
Freedom!

ACT THREE

SCENE ONE

A wild, rocky mountain, on a dark, silent night. After a few moments, a smuggler appears at the top of the rocks, then another, then two others, and finally twenty, climbing and scrambling down. Some carry heavy bales on their backs. Don José, Carmen, El Dancairo, El Remendado, Frasquita, and Mercedes enter with them.

CHORUS
Listen, comrades, there's a fortune
waiting for us down below.
But be careful as you go.
Don't make a false move.

CARMEN, DON JOSÉ, FRASQUITA,
MERCEDES, EL REMENDADO, EL DANCAIRO
This is good work,
if you've got heart and a strong will.
There's danger above,
there's danger below.
There's danger all around,
but who cares?
We'll keep going, no matter what.
Who cares about the storm?
Who cares about the thunder?
Who cares about the soldier
who's waiting to catch us below?
We'll just keep going on!

"There's danger all around, but who cares?"
Act Three

Listen, comrades, there's a fortune
waiting for us below.
But be careful as you go.
Don't make a false move.
Be careful!

EL DANCAIRO

Rest here an hour, my friends.
We'll go ahead to make sure the road is safe.
And that there won't be any trouble
about smuggling our goods into town.

CARMEN *(to Don José)*

What are you looking at?

DON JOSÉ

I was thinking that a kind, honest old woman
lives down there.
And she believes I'm an honest man.
Unfortunately, she's wrong!

CARMEN

And who is this woman?

DON JOSÉ

Carmen, don't make fun of me, I warn you!
Because she's my mother.

CARMEN

Fine. Then go back to her right now.
You know this life we lead isn't for you.
You should go away. The sooner, the better.

DON JOSÉ

Go away? We should separate?

CARMEN

Certainly!

"You know this life we lead isn't for you, Don José."
Act Three

DON JOSÉ
Separate? Carmen, if you say that once more . . .

CARMEN
You'll kill me, perhaps?
What a look!
And you don't have another word to say . . .
What do I care?
After all, fate decides everything.

(Carmen turns her back on Don José, and sits by Frasquita and Mercedes. Don José walks away, and lies down on the rocks. Mercedes and Frasquita shuffle cards, and spread them out on the ground.)

SCENE TWO

MERCEDES AND FRASQUITA
Shuffle the cards! Cut the deck!
Good, let's see now. Let's see.
Three cards here . . .
Four there . . .

Now talk to us, my beauties.
Tell us about the future.
Give us all the news.

Tell us who will betray us!
Tell us who will love us!
Speak! Speak!

FRASQUITA
Me, I see a young lover
Who's crazy for me.

MERCEDES
Mine is very rich, and very old.
But he's talking about marriage!

FRASQUITA
Mine gallops up on his horse
and carries me away into the mountains.

MERCEDES
Mine sets me up in a fabulous palace,
like royalty!

FRASQUITA
Mine makes passionate love to me,
night and day.

MERCEDES
Mine loads me down with gold,
diamonds, all sorts of precious jewels.

FRASQUITA
Mine becomes a famous leader.
A hundred men march at his orders.

MERCEDES
And mine? Mine?
Can I believe my eyes?
Yes. He dies!
I'm his widow! An heiress!

MERCEDES AND FRASQUITA

Talk to us again, my beauties.
Tell us about the future.
Give us all the news.

(They consult the cards again.)

FRASQUITA

Money!

MERCEDES

Love!

CARMEN

Let's see now. Let me have my turn.
(Carmen deals herself cards.)
A diamond! A spade!
Death! It's so clear.
First me, then him.
But for both of us . . . death.

It's useless to try to escape
the bitter truth.
You can shuffle the cards a dozen times.
It doesn't help.
The cards are honest. They never lie.
If fate smiles on you,
then shuffle and deal without a care.
Those lucky cards will keep turning up.
They'll announce your good luck.
But if you're to die, if your time has come,
it's sealed by fate.
Deal again twenty times,
The cards have no pity.
They'll keep on saying, "Death!"
Again! Again! Nothing but death!

MERCEDES AND FRASQUITA

Talk to us again, my beauties.
Tell us about the future.
Give us all the news.

CARMEN *(still dealing the cards)*
Again!

FRASQUITA
Tell us who will betray us.

MERCEDES
Tell us who will betray us.

CARMEN *(dealing the cards)*
Again!

FRASQUITA
Tell us who will love us.

MERCEDES
Tell us who will love us.

CARMEN
It's hopeless. Death. Death.
Nothing but death.

FRASQUITA AND MERCEDES
Tell us again, again!
Tell us who will betray us.

CARMEN
Death! Death!

FRASQUITA AND MERCEDES
Tell us who will love us.

CARMEN
Again! Again!
Nothing but death.

MERCEDES
Money!

FRASQUITA

Love!

CARMEN

Nothing but death!

CARMEN, FRASQUITA, MERCEDES

Again! Again! Again!

SCENE THREE

El Dancairo and El Remendado enter.

CARMEN

Well?

EL DANCAIRO

Well, we'll try to get through.
And we will get through!
You stay up there, José,
and guard our goods.

FRASQUITA

Is the road clear?

EL DANCAIRO

Yes, but watch out for surprises.
I saw three customs officers guarding the gap!
We'll have to get them away from there.

CARMEN

Pick up your packs, and let's go.
We have to get through.
And we will get through!

CARMEN, FRASQUITA, MERCEDES, GYPSY WOMEN
As for the customs officers,
just leave them to us.
They're all alike,
they'll want to please us.
And each will fancy himself a ladies' man.
So let us go first!
The customs officer will be easygoing.
He'll be gallant.
He'll be charming!

CARMEN, FRASQUITA, MERCEDES
He won't even put up a fight.
No, not if we just let him put his arm around us
and listen to his compliments.
And if we have to go as far as to smile,
what do you expect? We'll smile!

CARMEN, FRASQUITA, MERCEDES, GYPSY WOMEN
And I can assure you in advance,
we'll smuggle our goods right through!

FRASQUITA
Forward march!

MERCEDES
Forward march!

FRASQUITA
Let's go!

*(The smugglers pick up their bales, and exit, along with the women.
Don José, remaining behind as a guard, takes his rifle and exits over
the rocks. Micaela enters, looking about fearfully.)*

SCENE FOUR

MICAELA
This is where the smugglers hide out.
So I'll find José here.
And I'll do what his mother asked,
I'll do it without being afraid.

I say that nothing frightens me.
I say it, but it's not true.
It's useless to pretend to be brave
when deep in my heart,
I'm dying of fear.
I'm all alone
in this wild, deserted place.
I'm all alone, and I'm afraid.
But it's cowardly of me to be afraid.
Lord, You will give me courage
You will protect me, Lord.

I'm going to see that woman.
Her black magic turned the man
I once loved into a bandit.
She's dangerous. She's beautiful.
But I won't be afraid of her.
No, no, I'll won't be afraid.
I'll stand right up to her!

Lord, You will protect me.

(Don José enters on the rock above. He does not notice Micaela.)

MICAELA
If I'm not mistaken, that's him on the rock!
José! José!
I can't climb up there to him.
What is he doing?
He's going to shoot!
I overestimated my strength, dear God!

(As Micaela runs to hide behind a rock, Don José fires his rifle in the opposite direction. Escamillo enters, holding his hat in his hands. There is a bullet hole through it.)

ESCAMILLO
A little lower, and that would have been
the end of me.

DON JOSÉ
Who are you? Answer me!

ESCAMILLO
Easy there, my friend.
I'm Escamillo, the toreador from Grenada.

DON JOSÉ
Escamillo!

ESCAMILLO
That's me.

DON JOSÉ
I've heard of you. And you're welcome here.
But really, my friend, you should have stayed away.

ESCAMILLO
You may be right.
But I'm in love, my friend.
Madly in love!
And any man worth his salt
would risk his life for the woman he loved.

DON JOSÉ
The woman you love is here?

ESCAMILLO
Exactly. She's a gypsy, my friend.

DON JOSÉ
What's her name?

ESCAMILLO

Carmen.

DON JOSÉ *(aside)*

Carmen!

ESCAMILLO

She has a lover.
A soldier who deserted the army for her.

DON JOSÉ *(aside)*

Carmen!

ESCAMILLO

They were madly in love.
But that's over, I believe.
Carmen's love affairs never last
more than six months.

DON JOSÉ

You love her in spite of that?

ESCAMILLO

I love her!

DON JOSÉ

You still love her, in spite of that?

ESCAMILLO

I love her, yes, my friend.
I love her. I love her madly.

DON JOSÉ

But any man who tries to carry off
one of our gypsy girls has to pay a price,
you know.

ESCAMILLO

Fine. Then I'll pay, I'll pay.

DON JOSÉ
The price is a knife-fight to the death!

ESCAMILLO *(surprised)*
A knife-fight!

DON JOSÉ
You understand?

ESCAMILLO
Oh, it's very clear.
That deserter, that handsome soldier she loves—
or at least, used to love—is you.

DON JOSÉ
Yes, it's me.

ESCAMILLO
I'm delighted to meet you, my friend.
Delighted. We've come full circle.

DON JOSÉ
At last I can pour out my anger.
I want blood! Yes, blood!
And let it flow soon.

ESCAMILLO
How foolish of me, I really should laugh.
To search out the mistress,
and find her lover!

DON JOSÉ AND ESCAMILLO
On guard! And fight for your life!
Too bad for the one who's slow
with his knife!
On guard! And fight for your life!

(They fight until Escamillo slips and falls. Don José is about to stab Escamillo when the gypsies enter, with Carmen. She rushes over and stops Don José.)

"On guard! And fight for your life!"
Act Three

CARMEN
Stop! Stop, José!

ESCAMILLO
Well! I'm delighted that it's you, Carmen,
who saved my life.
As for you, my handsome soldier, we're even.
And we'll fight for this beauty again,
whenever you chose the day.

EL DANCAIRO
Come on, come on, no more quarreling.
We have to leave.
(to Escamillo)
Good night to you, my friend.

ESCAMILLO
Before saying good-bye, at least allow me
to invite all of you to the bullfight
in Seville.
I expect to be at my very best.
And whoever loves me will come.
(to Don José)
My friend, calm down.
I've finished for now.
(to Carmen)
Yes, I've finished for now.
There's nothing to add but my fondest farewell.

(Escamillo exits slowly. Don José is held back by El Dancairo and El Remendado.)

DON JOSÉ *(to Carmen)*
Watch yourself, Carmen!
I've had enough!

(Carmen shrugs her shoulders indifferently and walks away from him.)

EL DANCAIRO
Get going, get going. We have to leave.

GYPSIES

Get going, get going. We have to leave.

EL REMENDADO

Stop! There's someone hiding behind that rock!

(He goes behind the rock, and re-enters with Micaela.)

CARMEN

A woman!

EL DANCAIRO

Good Lord! What a nice surprise!

DON JOSÉ

Micaela!

MICAELA

Don José!

DON JOSÉ

Poor girl, what are you doing here?

MICAELA

I came to find you.
Down in the valley, there's a cottage
where someone is praying for you.
A mother. Your mother.
She's weeping, poor woman. For her son.
She's weeping, and calling for you.
She's weeping, and holding out her arms to you.
Take pity on her, José.
José, come with me, come with me.

CARMEN

Go on, go on. You should go back.
This life of ours isn't for you.

DON JOSÉ

You're telling me to leave
so you can run after your new lover!

No, no, you won't.
Even if it costs me my life,
no, Carmen,
I'll never leave you!
And the chain that binds us together
will bind us to the death!
No, no, I won't leave you.

MICAELA *(to Don José)*
Listen to me, I beg you.
Your mother is holding
    out her arms to you.
You can break the
    chain that binds
    you, José.

EL DANCAIRO, EL REMENDADO, GYPSIES
If you don't go, José, it'll cost
    you your life.
The chain that binds
    you will be
    snapped by
    your death.

DON JOSÉ *(to Micaela)*
Leave me!

MICAELA
José!

DON JOSÉ
I'm doomed.

GYPSIES
José, watch out!

DON JOSÉ *(to Carmen)*
I'm holding on to you, damn you!
I'm holding on to you, and I'll force you
to follow our destiny!

Your fate and mine are one and the same.
Even if it costs me my life,
no, I won't leave you!

GYPSIES
Watch out! Watch out, Don José!

MICAELA
One more word. It will be my last.
José, your mother is dying.
And your mother doesn't want to die
without seeing you, and forgiving you.

DON JOSÉ
My mother! She's dying!

MICAELA
Yes, Don José.

DON JOSÉ
Let's leave! Let's leave!
(to Carmen)
Are you satisfied? I'm leaving.
But we'll meet again!

(Don José leads Micaela away. He hears Escamillo's voice, stops and hesitates.)

ESCAMILLO *(from the distance)*
Toreador, on guard!
Toreador! Toreador!
And as you fight, yes,
dream of the dark eyes watching you.
And of the love that's waiting for you, toreador.
The love, the love that's waiting for you.

(Don José exits with Micaela. The gypsies pick up their bundles and bales and exit with Carmen.)

ACT FOUR

SCENE ONE

A square in Seville. At the back are the walls of the ancient arena. The entrance is covered by a long canvas. The square is full of people waiting for the procession that precedes the bullfight. Vendors are selling a variety of goods.

VENDORS
Two pesetas! Only two pesetas!
Four pesetas! Only four pesetas!
Fans for sale! Cool yourselves off!
Juicy oranges to eat!
Buy a program, with all the details!
Wine for sale!
Water for sale!
Cigarettes for sale!

(Zuniga and another officer enter, escorting Mercedes and Frasquita.)

ZUNIGA *(to a woman vendor)*
Some oranges. Quick!

VARIOUS WOMEN VENDORS *(to Frasquita and Mercedes)*
Here they are. Help yourselves, ladies.

(Zuniga pays one vendor)

WOMAN VENDOR
Thank you, Officer, thank you!

"Juicy oranges to eat! Only two pesetas!"
Act Four

OTHER VENDORS *(to Zuniga)*
Take these, Señor, they're better.

VENDORS
Fans for sale! Oranges to eat!
A program with all the details!
Wine for sale!
Water for sale!
Cigarettes for sale!

ZUNIGA
Say! Give me two fans!

(A gypsy approaches Zuniga, and holds up a pair of glasses.)

GYPSY *(to Zuniga)*
Do you want a pair of glasses?

(Zuniga pushes the gypsy aside. The vendors continue to hawk their wares. A group of children enters in excitement. Loud fanfare is heard from off stage.)

CHILDREN
Here they come, here they come!
Here comes the cuadrilla!

CROWD
Here they come! Yes, here they come!
The cuadrilla!

CHILDREN AND CROWD
Here they come!
The cuadrilla of toreros!
Their lances sparkle in the sun.
Let's toss our hats in the air!
Up in the air, to cheer them on!

Here they are! Here they are!
The cuadrilla of toreros!

(The ceremonial procession preceding the bullfight begins to enter the arena. The onlookers comment as the procession, led by a constable, passes by them.)

> Look who's marching into the square.
> Right ahead of everyone, just marching along.
> The constable with his ugly face!
> Throw him out, throw him out!

(The chulos and banderilleros pass.)

> Let's all give a cheer for the brave chulos!
> Hurrah! Three cheers for their courage!
>
> See? The banderilleros!
> Just look at their swagger.
> Look! How proud they are,
> all dressed up for the fight
> in bright, shining, embroidered costumes.
> The banderilleros are here!

(The picadors enter.)

> Another cuadrilla is coming!
> Look, the picadors!
> Oh, how handsome they look!
> They can't wait to goad the bull
> with the tips of their lances.
> Here comes the greatest of all!
> The matador!

(At last Escamillo enters with Carmen, who is radiant with pride and delight and is dressed in brilliant, gaudy colors.)

CROWD
> Escamillo! Escamillo!
> It's the matador with his sword
> who always steals the show.
> He comes in at the end
> and strikes the final blow.
> Hurrah for Escamillo! Hurrah!

ESCAMILLO *(to Carmen)*
If you love me, Carmen, then very soon
you'll be proud of me.
If you love me, if you truly love me . . .

CARMEN
Oh, I do love you, Escamillo.
I love you. May I be struck dead
if I've ever loved anyone as I love you.

CARMEN AND ESCAMILLO
Oh, I love you. Yes, I love you.

(A group of constables pushes the crowd back.)

CONSTABLES
Move back! Move back! Make way for our Mayor!

(The Mayor enters, accompanied by guards, and exits into the arena, followed by the constables. Meanwhile, Frasquita and Mercedes draw Carmen aside.)

FRASQUITA

Carmen, take my advice.
Don't stay here.

CARMEN

And why not, may I ask?

MERCEDES

He's here!

CARMEN

Who is?

MERCEDES

Him! Don José!
He's hiding in the crowd. Look!

(Carmen sees Don José in the crowd.)

CARMEN

Yes, I see him.

FRASQUITA

Be careful!

CARMEN

He can't frighten a woman like me.
I'll wait for him and talk to him.

MERCEDES

Carmen, believe me, you'd better be careful!

CARMEN

I'm not afraid of anyone!

FRASQUITA

Be careful!

(The procession has gone into the arena, followed by the crowd. Don José remains. Frasquita and Mercedes now exit into the arena, leaving Carmen alone with Don José.)

S C E N E   T W O

C A R M E N

It's you!

D O N   J O S É

It's me.

C A R M E N

They warned me that you were nearby,
that you would be coming here.
They even said I should fear for my life.
But I'm no coward.
I would never run away.

D O N   J O S É

I'm not threatening you.
I'm pleading with you.
Our past, Carmen, our quarrels . . .
I've forgotten them.
Yes, the two of us are going to
start a new life, far away from here,
under a different sky.

C A R M E N

What you're asking is impossible!
Carmen has never lied.
Nothing can change her mind.
Everything is over between us.

(Don José looks shocked.)

D O N   J O S É

Carmen, there's still time.
Yes, there's still time.
Oh, my Carmen, let me save you.
I adore you.
Oh, let me save you,
and save myself as well.

CARMEN

No! I know very well that my time has come.
I know very well that you'll kill me.
But whether I live or die . . .
no, no, I'll never give in to you!

DON JOSÉ

Carmen, there's still time.
Yes, there's still time.
Oh, my Carmen, let me save you.
I adore you.
Oh, let me save you,
and save myself as well.

CARMEN

Why are you still trying to win
a heart that's no longer yours?
It's useless to tell me, "I love you."
You'll never get anything from me.

DON JOSÉ

Then you don't love me anymore?
You don't love me anymore?

CARMEN

No. I don't love you anymore.

DON JOSÉ

But, Carmen, I still love you.
Carmen, I still adore you!

CARMEN

What good are all these useless words?

DON JOSÉ

Carmen, I love you, I adore you!
All right, if I have to—to please you—
I'll even be a bandit again. Anything you want.
Anything! Do you hear me? Anything!
But don't leave me, my Carmen.
Oh, remember how happy we once were,

how we loved each other, not long ago.
Don't leave me, Carmen, don't leave me!

CARMEN

Carmen will never give in.
She was born free,
and she will die free!

CROWD *(off stage in the arena)*

Hurrah! Hurrah! What a bullfight!
The sand is red with blood.
And the bull? The bull is charging!
Look, look!
They're goading the bull,
he's running, he's charging!
Look!
He's been struck right through the heart!
Victory!

(Carmen and Don José have been silent, listening to the crowd. At the shout "Victory!" a sigh of delight escapes Carmen's lips. Don José's eyes are fixed upon her. She takes a step toward the arena. Don José blocks her way.)

DON JOSÉ

Where are you going?

CARMEN

Leave me alone.

DON JOSÉ

That man they're cheering
is your new lover!

CARMEN

Let me go, let me go!

DON JOSÉ

I swear I won't let you go to him, Carmen.
You'll leave here with me!

"The bull's been struck right through the heart!"
Act Four

CARMEN

Let me go, Don José. I'll never go with you!

DON JOSÉ

Are you saying you're going to meet him?
Then you love him?

CARMEN

I love him!
I love him and even in the face of death,
I'll repeat that I love him!

(Again, Carmen tries to enter the arena, but is held back by Don José. Fanfare and cheering are heard from the arena.)

DON JOSÉ *(violently)*

I gave up my honor, my very soul, because of you.
So that you can run to your lover, you slut!
And laugh at me, in his arms!
No, I swear on my life, you won't go to him.
Carmen, you're coming with me!

CARMEN

No, no, never!

DON JOSÉ

I'm tired of warning you.

CARMEN

Very well.
Strike me down, or let me pass!

DON JOSÉ

I'm asking you for the last time, you demon!
Are you coming with me?

CARMEN

No, no!

(Carmen tears a ring from her finger and throws it at Don José.)

You once gave me this ring.
Take it back!

DON JOSÉ *(rushing at Carmen)*
Damn you!

(As the fanfare and cheering continue from off stage, Carmen tries to escape. But Don José draws a knife, and seizes her at the entrance of the arena.)

CROWD *(off stage)*
Toreador, on guard! Toreador! Toreador!
And as you fight, yes,
dream of those dark eyes watching you.
And of the love that's waiting for you, Toreador.
The love, the love that's waiting for you!

(Don José stabs Carmen, who falls dead. As the crowd enters from the arena, constables approach Don José.)

DON JOSÉ
You can arrest me.
I'm the man who killed her.

(Escamillo appears in the entrance of the arena. Don José throws himself on Carmen's body.)

DON JOSÉ
Oh, Carmen! My Carmen! My love!

"I gave up my honor, my very soul, because of you."
Act Four

CARMEN

Libretto en Français

ACTE PREMIER

SCÈNE 1

Grande place à Séville. A droite, la porte de la manufacture de tabac. Au fond, face au public, pont praticable. De la scène on arrive à ce pont par un escalier tournant qui fait sa révolution à droite au-dessus de la porte de la manufacture de tabac. A gauche, le corps de garde.

Au lever du rideau, une quinzaine de soldats, Dragons du régiment d'Almanza, sont groupés devant le corps de garde. Mouvement de passants sur la place.

CHOEUR DES SOLDATS
Sur la place
Chacun passe,
Chacun vient, chacun va;
Drôles de gens que ces gens-là.

MORALÈS
A la porte du corps de garde,
Pour tuer le temps,
On fume, on jase, l'on regarde
Passer les passants.

(Micaela est entrée. Hésitante, embarrassée, elle regarde les soldats avance, recule.)

MORALÈS *(aux soldats)*
Regardez donc cette petite
Qui semble vouloir nous parler.
Voyez, elle tourne, elle hésite.

LES SOLDATS
A son secours il faut aller.

MORALÈS *(à Micaela)*
Que cherchez-vous, la belle?

MICAELA
Moi, je cherche un brigadier.

MORALÈS
Je suis là! Voilà!

MICAELA
Mon brigadier, à moi, s'appelle
Don José, le connaissez-vous?

MORALÈS
Don José, nous le connaissons tous.

MICAELA
Est-il avec vous, je vous prie?

MORALÈS
Il n'est pas brigadier dans notre compagnie.

MICAELA *(désolée)*
Alors il n'est pas là.

MORALÈS
Non, ma charmante, il n'est pas là,
Mais tout à l'heure il y sera.
Il y sera quand la garde montante
Remplacera la garde descendante.

LES SOLDATS
Il y sera quand la garde montante
Remplacera la garde descendante.

MORALÈS

Mais en attendant qu'il vienne,
Voulez-vous, la belle enfant,
Voulez-vous prendre la peine
D'entrer chez nous un instant?

MICAELA

Chez vous!

LES SOLDATS

Chez nous.

MICAELA

Non pas, non pas.
Grand merci, messieurs les soldats.

MORALÈS

Entrez sans crainte, mignonne,
Je vous promets qu'on aura,
Pour votre chère personne,
Tous les égards qu'il faudra.

MICAELA

Je n'en doute pas; cependant
Je reviendrai, c'est plus prudent.
(Reprenant en riant la phrase du Sergent.)
Je reviendrai quand la garde montante
Remplacera la garde descendante.

LES SOLDATS ET MORALÈS *(entourant Micaela)*

Il faut rester car la garde montante
Va remplacer la garde descendante.

MORALÈS

Vous resterez.

MICAELA

Non pas! non pas!
Au revoir messieurs les soldats.

(Elle s'échappe et se sauve en courant.)

MORALÈS

L'oiseau s'envole,
On s'en console.
Reprenons notre passe-temps,
Et regardons passer les gens.

LES SOLDATS

Sur la place.
Chacun passe,
Chacun vient, chacun va;
Drôles de gens que ces gens-là.

SCÈNE 2

On entend au loin, une marche militaire, clairons et fifres. C'est la garde montante qui arrive. Un officier sort du poste. Les soldats du poste vont prendre leurs lances et se rangent en ligne devant le corps de garde. La marche militaire se rapproche, se rapproche. La garde montante débouche enfin venant de la gauche et traverse le pont. Deux clairons et deux fifres d'abord. Puis une bande de petits gamins. Derrière les enfants, le lieutenant Zuniga et le brigadier Don José, puis les Dragons avec leurs lances.

CHOEUR DES GAMINS

Avec la garde montante.
Nous arrivons, nous voilà.
Sonne, trompette éclatante,
Tara ta ta, tara ta ta;
Nous marchons, la tête haute
Comme de petits soldats,
Marquant sans faire de faute
Une, deux, marquant le pas.
Les épaules en arrière
Et la poitrine en dehors,
Les bras de cette manière
Tombant tout le long du corps;
Avec la garde montante
Nous arrivons, nous voilà.

Sonne, trompette éclatante,
Tara ta ta, tara ta ta.

(La garde montante va se ranger à droite en face de la garde descendante. Les officiers se saluent de l'épée et se mettent à causer à voix basse. On relève les sentinelles.)

MORALÈS
Une jeune fille charmante
Vient de nous demander
Si tu n'étais pas là. Jupe
Bleue et natte tombante.

DON JOSÉ
Ce doit être Micaela.

(La garde descendante passe devant la garde montante. Les gamins en troupe reprennent la place qu'ils occupaient derrière les tambours et les fifres de la garde montante.)

REPRISE DU CHŒUR DES GAMINS
Et la garde descendante
Rentre chez elle et s'en va.
Sonne, trompette éclatante,
Tara ta ta, tara ta ta.
Nous marchons la tête haute
Comme de petits soldats,
Marquant, sans faire de faute,
Une . . . deux . . . marquant le pas.
Tara ta ta, tara ta ta.

(Soldats, gamins et curieux s'éloignent par le fond; chœur, fifres et clairons, vont diminuant. L'officier de la garde montante, pendant ce temps, passe silencieusement l'inspection de ses hommes. Les Dragons rentrent dans le corps de garde. Don José et le lieutenant restent seuls en scène.)

ZUNIGA
C'est bien là, n'est-ce pas, dans ce grand bâtiment
Que travaillent les cigarières?

DON JOSÉ

C'est là mon officier, et bien certainement
On ne vit nulle part, filles aussi légères.

ZUNIGA

Mais au moins sont elles jolies?

DON JOSÉ

Mon officier, je n'en sais rien,
Et m'occupe assez peu de ces galanteries.

ZUNIGA

Ce qui t'occupe ami,
Je le sais bien,
Une jeune fille charmante,
Qu'on appelle Micaela,
Jupe bleue et natte tombante.
Tu ne réponds rien à cela?

DON JOSÉ

Je réponds que c'est vrai,
Je réponds que je l'aime!
Quant aux ouvrières d'ici,
Quant à leur beauté, les voici!
Et vous pouvez juger vous même.

(La place se remplit de jeunes gens qui viennent se placer sur le passage des cigarières. Les soldats sortent du poste. Don José s'assied sur une chaise, et reste là fort indifférent à toutes ces allées et venues, travaillant à son épinglette.)

JEUNES GENS

La cloche a sonné, nous, des ouvrières
Nous venons ici guetter le retour;
Et nous vous suivrons, brunes cigarières,
En vous murmurant des propos d'amour.

(A ce moment paraissent les cigarières, la cigarette aux lèvres. Elles passent sous le pont et descendent lentement en scène.)

LES SOLDATS

Voyez-les. Regards impudents,
Mines coquettes,
Fumant toutes du bout des dents
La cigarette.

LES CIGARIÈRES

Dans l'air, nous suivons des yeux
La fumée,
Qui vers les cieux
Monte, monte parfumée.
Dans l'air nous suivons des yeux
La fumée.
Cela monte doucement
A la tête,
Tout doucement cela vous met
L'âme en fête,
Dans l'air nous suivons des yeux
La fumée,
Etc.
Le doux parler des amants
C'est fumée;
Leurs transports et leurs serments
C'est fumée.
Dans l'air nous suivons des yeux
La fumée,
Etc.

LES SOLDATS

Mais nous ne voyons pas la Carmencita.

LES SOLDATS ET LES JEUNES GENS

La voilà,
La voilà,
Voilà la Carmencita.

(Entre Carmen. Elle a un bouquet de cassie à son corsage et une fleur de cassie dans le coin de la bouche.)

LES JEUNES GENS *(entrés avec Carmen)*

Carmen, sur tes pas, nous nous pressons tous;

Carmen, sois gentille, au moins réponds nous
Et dis-nous quel jour tu nous aimeras.

CARMEN *(les regardant)*
Quand je vous aimerai? Ma foi, je ne sais pas.
Peut-être jamais, peut-être demain;
Mais pas aujourd'hui, c'est certain.

L'amour est un oiseau rebelle
Que nul ne peut apprivoiser,
Et c'est bien en vain qu'on l'appelle,
S'il lui convient de refuser.
Rien n'y fait; menace ou prière,
L'un parle bien, l'autre se tait;
Et c'est l'autre que je préfère,
Il n'a rien dit mais il me plait.
L'amour est enfant de Bohême,
Il n'a jamais connu de loi;
Si tu ne m'aimes pas, je t'aime;
Si je t'aime, prends garde à toi.
L'oiseau que tu croyais surprendre
Battit de l'aile et s'envola—
L'amour est loin, tu peux l'attendre;
Tu ne l'attends plus—il est là.
Tout autour de toi, vite, vite,
Il vient, s'en va, puis il revient—
Tu crois le tenir, il t'évite,
Tu veux l'éviter, il te tient.
L'amour est enfant de Bohême,
Il n'a jamais connu de loi;
Si tu ne m'aimes pas, je t'aime;
Si je t'aime, prends garde à toi.

JEUNES GENS
Carmen, sur tes pas, nous nous pressons tous;
Carmen, sois gentille, au moins réponds-nous.

(Moment de silence. Les jeunes gens entourent Carmen; celle-ci les regarde l'un après l'autre, sort du cercle qu'ils forment autour d'elle et s'en va droit à Don José qui est toujours occupé de son épinglette.)

CARMEN

Eh! compère, qu'est-ce que tu fais là?

DON JOSÉ

Je fais une chaîne pour attacher mon épinglette.

CARMEN *(riant)*

Ton épinglette, vraiment! Ton épinglette—épinglier
de mon âme.

*(Elle arrache de son corsage la fleur de cassie et la lance à Don
José. Il se lève brusquement. Éclat de rire général; la cloche de la
manufacture sonne une deuxième fois. Sortie des ouvrières et des
jeunes gens sur la reprise.)*

LES CIGARIÈRES

L'amour est enfant de Bohême.
Il n'a jamais connu de loi;
Si tu ne m'aimes pas, je t'aime;
Si je t'aime, prends garde à toi.

DON JOSÉ

Quels regards! Quelle effronterie!
Cette fleur la m'a fait
L'effet d'une balle qui m'arrivait!
Le parfum en est fort et la fleur est jolie!
Et la femme . . .
S'il est vraiment des sorcières,
C'en est une certainement.

MICAELA

José!

DON JOSÉ

Micaela!

MICAELA

Me voici!

DON JOSÉ

Quelle joie!

MICAELA

C'est votre mère qui m'envoie!

DON JOSÉ

Parle-moi de ma mère.

MICAELA

J'apporte de sa part, fidèle messagère,
Cette lettre.

DON JOSÉ *(regardant la lettre)*
Une lettre!

MICAELA

Et puis un peu d'argent
(Elle lui remet une petite bourse.)
Pour ajouter à votre traitement,
Et puis—

DON JOSÉ

Et puis?

MICAELA

Et puis—vraiment je n'ose,
Et puis—encore une autre chose
Qui vaut mieux que l'argent et qui,
    pour un bon fils,
Aura sans doute plus de prix.

DON JOSÉ

Cette autre chose, quelle est-elle?
Parle donc.

MICAELA

Oui, je parlerai;
Ce que l'on m'a donné, je vous le donnerai.
Votre mère avec moi sortait de la chapelle,
Et c'est alors qu'en m'embrassant,
"Tu vas," m'a-t-elle dit, "t'en aller à la ville;
La route n'est pas longue, une fois à Séville,
Tu chercheras mon fils, mon José, mon enfant.

Et tu lui diras que sa mère
Songe nuit et jour à l'absent,
Qu'elle regrette et qu'elle espère,
Qu'elle pardonne et qu'elle attend;
Tout cela, n'est-ce pas? mignonne,
De ma part tu le lui diras,
Et ce baiser que je te donne
De ma part tu le lui rendras."

DON JOSÉ *(très ému)*
Un baiser pour son fils.

MICAELA
José, je vous le rends, comme je l'ai promis.

(Micaela se hausse un peu sur la pointe des pieds et donne à Don José un baiser bien franc, bien maternel. Don José, tres ému, la laisse faire. Il la regarde bien dans les yeux. Un moment de silence.)

DON JOSÉ
Ma mère, je la vois, oui, je revois mon village.
O souvenirs d'autrefois! Doux souvenirs du pays!
Vous remplissez mon coeur de force et de courage
O souvenirs chéris,
Souvenirs d'autrefois! souvenirs du pays!

DON JOSÉ ET MICAELA
Ma mère, je la vois, etc.
Sa mère, il la revoit, etc.

DON JOSÉ *(les yeux fixés sur la manufacture)*
Qui sait de quel démon j'allais être la proie!
Même de loin, ma mère me défend,
Et ce baiser qu'elle m'envoie
Écarte le péril et sauve son enfant,

MICAELA
Quel démon? Quel péril? Je ne comprends pas
   bien.

Que veut dire cela?

DON JOSÉ

Rien! Rien!
Parlons de toi, la messagère.
Tu vas retourner au pays?

MICAELA

Ce soir même, et demain je verrai votre mère.

DON JOSÉ

Eh bien, tu lui diras
Que son fils l'aime et la vénère,
Et qu'il se repent aujourd'hui.
Il veut que là-bas sa mère
Soit contente de lui!
Tout cela, n'est-ce pas, mignonne,
De ma part tu le lui diras;
Et ce baiser que je te donne,
De ma part tu le lui rendras.

(Il l'embrasse.)

MICAELA

Oui je vous le promets de la part de son fils.
José je le rendrai comme je l'ai promis.

DON JOSÉ

Ma mère, je la vois, etc.

MICAELA

Sa mère, il la revoit, etc.

DON JOSÉ

Reste là maintenant,
Pendant que je lirai.

MICAELA

Non pas, lisez d'abord,
Et puis je reviendrai.

DON JOSÉ
Pourquoi t'en aller?

MICAELA
C'est plus sage,
Cela me convient d'avantage.
Lisez! puis je reviendrai.

DON JOSÉ
Tu reviendras?

MICAELA
Je reviendrai!

DON JOSÉ
Ne crains rien, ma mère, ton fils t'obéira,
Fera ce que tu lui dis; j'aime Micaela,
Je la prendrai pour femme,
Quant à tes fleurs, sorcière infâme!

(Au moment où il va arracher les fleurs de sa veste, grande rumeur dans l'intérieur de la manufacture. Entre le lieutenant suivi des soldats.)

LE LIEUTENANT
Que se passe-t-il donc là-bas?

(Les ouvrières sortent rapidement et en désordre.)

CHOEUR
Au secours! n'entendez-vous pas?
Au secours, messieurs les soldats!

PREMIER GROUPE DE FEMMES
C'est la Carmencita.

DEUXIÈME GROUPE DE FEMMES
Non, non, ce n'est pas elle!

PREMIER GROUPE
C'est elle.

DEUXIÈME GROUPE
Pas du tout.

PREMIER GROUPE
Si fait! C'est elle
Elle a porté les premiers coups.

TOUTES LES FEMMES *(entourant le lieutenant)*
Ne les écoutez pas, monsieur,
Ecoutez-nous,
Ecoutez-nous.

DEUXIÈME GROUPE
(Elles tirent l'officier de leur côté)
La Manuelita disait
Et répétait à voix haute
Qu'elle achèterait sans faute
Un âne qui lui plaisait.

PREMIER GROUPE
Alors la Carmencita
Railleuse à son ordinaire,
Dit: "un âne, pourquoi faire?
Un balai te suffira."

DEUXIÈME GROUPE
Manuelita riposta
Et dit à sa camarade:
"Pour certaine promenade
Mon âne te servira.

PREMIER GROUPE
Et ce jour-là tu pourras
A bon droit faire la fière;
Deux laquais suivront derrière,
T'émouchant à tour de bras."

TOUTES LES FEMMES
Là-dessus toutes les deux
Se sont prises aux cheveux.

LE LIEUTENANT
Au diable tout ce bavardage!
(à Don José)
Prenez, José, deux hommes avec vous
Et voyez là-dedans qui cause ce tapage.

(Don José prend deux hommes avec lui. Les soldats entrent dans la manufacture. Pendant ce temps les femmes se pressent, se disputent entre elles.)

PREMIER GROUPE
C'est la Carmencita.

DEUXIÈME GROUPE
Non, non, écoutez, nous, etc., etc.

LE LIEUTENANT *(assourdi)*
Holà! holà!
Eloignez-moi toutes ces femmes-là.

TOUTES LES FEMMES
Ecoutez-nous! écoutez-nous!

(Les soldats repoussent les femmes et les écartent. Carmen parait sur la porte de la manufacture amenée par Don José et suivie par deux dragons.)

DON JOSÉ
Mon officier, c'était une querelle;
Des injures d'abord, puis à la fin des coups,
Une femme blessée.

LE LIEUTENANT
Et par qui?

DON JOSÉ
Mais par elle.

LE LIEUTENANT
Vous entendez, que nous répondrez vous?

CARMEN

Tra la la la la la la la,
Coupe-moi, brûle-moi,
Je ne te dirai rien;
Tra la la la la la la la,
Je brave tout, le feu, le fer, et le ciel même!

LE LIEUTENANT

Fais-nous grâce de tes chansons,
Et puisque l'on t'a dit de répondre, réponds!

CARMEN

Tra la la la la la la la,
Mon secret, je le garde et je le garde bien!
Tra la la la la la la la,
J'en aime un autre et meurs en disant que je
    l'aime!

LE LIEUTENANT

Puisque tu le prends sur ce ton,
Tu chanteras ton air aux tours de la prison.

CHOEUR

En prison! en prison!

(Carmen veut se précipiter sur les femmes. Les soldats font évacuer la place.)

LE LIEUTENANT

Décidément vous avez la main leste!

CARMEN

Tra la la la la la la la

LE LIEUTENANT

C'est dommage,
C'est grand dommage,
Car elle est gentille vraiment!
Mais il faut bien la rendre sage,
Attachez ces deux jolis bras.

(Zuniga et les soldats entrent dans le corps de garde.)

CARMEN
Où me conduirez-vous?

DON JOSÉ
A la prison; et je n'y puis rien faire.

CARMEN
Vraiment? tu n'y peux rien faire?

DON JOSÉ
Non, rien! j'obéis à mes chefs.

CARMEN
Eh bien moi, je sais bien qu'en dépit de tes chefs
      eux-mêmes
Tu feras tout ce que je veux,
Et cela parce-que tu m'aimes!

DON JOSÉ
Moi, t'aimer?

CARMEN
Oui, José.
La fleur dont je t'ai fait présent,
Tu sais, la fleur de la sorciére,
Tu peux la jeter maintenant,
Le charme opère!

DON JOSÉ
Ne me parle plus! Tu m'entends!
Ne parle plus. Je le défends!

CARMEN
Près des remparts de Séville,
Chez mon ami Lillas Pastia,
J'irai danser la séguedille
Et boire du Manzanilla!
Oui, mais toute seule on s'ennuie,

Et les vrais plaisirs sont à deux . . .
Donc pour me tenir compagnie,
J'emmènerai mon amoureux.
Mon amoureux! . . . il est au diable . . .
Je l'ai mis à la porte hier . . .
Mon pauvre coeur très consolable,
Mon coeur est libre comme l'air . . .
J'ai des galants à la douzaine
Mais ils ne sont pas à mon gré:
Voici la fin de la semaine,
Qui veut m'aimer? je l'aimerai,
Qui veut mon âme? elle est à prendre
Vous arrivez au bon moment,
Je n'ai guère le temps d'attendre,
Car avec mon nouvel amant . . .
Près des remparts de Séville,
Chez mon ami Lillas Pastia,
J'irai danser la séguedille
Et boire du Manzanilla.

DON JOSÉ

Tais-toi, je t'avais dit de ne pas me parler!

CARMEN

Je ne te parle pas,
Je chante pour moi-même
Et je pense . . . il n'est pas défendu de penser,
Je pense à certain officier,
A certain officier qui m'aime,
Et qu'à mon tour je pourrais bien aimer . . .

DON JOSÉ

Carmen!

CARMEN

Mon officier n'est pas un capitaine,
Pas même un lieutenant, il n'est que brigadier:
Mais c'est assez pour une bohémienne,
Et je daigne m'en contenter!

DON JOSÉ

Carmen. Je suis comme un homme ivre,
Si je cède, si je me livre,
Ta promesse, tu la tiendras.
Si je t'aime, tu m'aimeras?

CARMEN

Oui . . .

DON JOSÉ

Chez Lillas Pastia . . .

CARMEN

Nous danserons la séguedille . . .

DON JOSÉ

Tous le promets! Carmen!

CARMEN

. . . et boirons du Manzanilla.

DON JOSÉ

Tous le promets!

(Déliant la corde qui attache les mains de Carmen.)

CARMEN

Près des remparts de Séville,
Chez mon ami Lillas Pastia,
Nous danserons la séguedille
Et boirons du Manzanilla.

(Rentre le lieutenant.)

ZUNIGA

Voici l'ordre, partez et faites bonne garde.

CARMEN *(bas à José)*

Sur le chemin je te pousserai aussi
fort que je le pourrai . . .

Laisse-toi renverser . . . le reste me regarde!

(à Zuniga)

L'amour est enfant de Bohême.
Il n'a jamais connu de loi;
Si tu ne m'aimes pas, je t'aime
Si je t'aime, prends garde à toi.

(En arrivant à l'entrée du pont à droite, Carmen pousse José qui se laisse renverser. Confusion, désordre, Carmen s'enfuit.)

ACTE DEUXIEME

SCÈNE 1

La taverne de Lillas Pastia. Carmen, Mercédès, Frasquita, le lieutenant Zuniga, Moralès et un lieutenant: C'est la fin d'un diner. La table est en désordre. Les officiers et les Bohémiennes fument des cigarettes. Deux Bohémiens râclent de la guitare dans un coin de la taverne et deux Bohémiennes, au milieu de la scène, dansent.

CARMEN

Les tringles des sistres tintaient
Avec un éclat métallique,
Et sur cette étrange musique
Les Zingarellas se levaient.
Tambours de basque allaient leur train,
Et les guitares forcenées
Grinçaient sous des mains obstinées
Même chanson, même refrain,
Tra la la la la la.

(Sur le refrain les Bohémiennes dansent.)

Les anneaux de cuivre et d'argent
Reluisaient sur les peaux bistrées;
D'orange ou de rouge zébrées
Les étoffes flottaient au vent—
La danse au chant se marait,
D'abord indécise et timide,
Plus vive ensuite et plus rapide,
Cela montait, montait, montait!
Tra la la la la la.

Les Bohémiens à tour de bras,
De leurs instruments faisaient rage,
Et cet éblouissant tapage,
Ensorcelait les Zingaras!
Sous le rhythme de la chanson,
Ardentes, folles, enfiévrées,
Elles se laissaient, enivrées,
Emporter par le tourbillon!
Tra la la la la la.

(Mouvement de danse très rapide, très violent. Carmen elle-même danse et vient, avec les dernières notes de l'orchestre, tomber haletante sur un banc de la taverne.)

FRASQUITA
Messieurs, Pastia me dit—

ZUNIGA
Que nous veut-il encor, maître Pastia?

FRASQUITA
Il dit que le Corrégidor veut que l'on ferme
l'auberge.

ZUNIGA
Eh bien! nous partirons.
Vous viendrez avec nous?

FRASQUITA
Non pas! nous, nous restons.

ZUNIGA
Et toi, Carmen, tu ne viens pas?
Ecoute! Deux mots dits tout bas:
Tu m'en veux.

CARMEN
Vous en vouloir! pourquoi?

ZUNIGA
Ce soldat, l'autre jour, emprisonné pour toi.

CARMEN
Qu' à-t'on fait de ce malheureux?

ZUNIGA
Maintenant il est libre!

CARMEN, FRASQUITA, MERCÉDÈS
Bonsoir messieurs nos amoureux!

(La scène est interrompue par un choeur chante dans la coulisse.)

CHOEUR
Vivat! vivat le Toréro!
Vivat! vivat Escamillo!

ZUNIGA
Une promenade aux flambeaux!
C'est le vainqueur des courses de Grenade,
Voulez-vous avec nous boire mon camarade,
A vos succès anciens, à vos succès nouveaux!

(Paraît Escamillo et son entourage.)

CHOEUR
Vivat! vivat! le Toréro! Vivat! vivat! Escamillo!

ESCAMILLO
Votre toast . . . je peux vous le rendre,
Señors, car avec les soldats
Oui, les Toréros peuvent s'entendre,

Pour plaisirs ils ont les combats.
Le cirque est plein, c'est jour de fête,
Le cirque est plein du haut en bas.
Les spectateurs perdant la tête,
S'interpellent à grand fracas;
Apostrophes, cris et tapage
Poussés jusques à la fureur,
Car c'est la fête du courage,
C'est la fête des gens de coeur!
Allons, en garde, ah
Toréador, en garde, Toréador, Toréador.
Et songe bien, oui songe en combattant
Qu'un oeil noir te regarde
Et que l'amour t'attend, Toréador.
L'amour t'attend.

FRASQUITA ET MERCÉDÈS

Toréador, en garde, Toréador, Toréador.
Et songe bien, oui songe en combattant
Qu'un oeil noir te regarde
Et que l'amour t'attend, Toréador.
L'amour t'attend.

ESCAMILLO

Tout d'un coup, on fait silence.
On fait silence, ah que se passe-t-il?
Plus de cris, c'est l'instant!
Le taureau s'élance
En bondissant hors du Toril!
Il s'élance! Il entre, il frappe!
Un cheval roule, entraînant un Picador,
"Ah! bravo! Toro!" hurle la foule,
Le taureau va . . . il vient . . . et frappe encor!
En secouant ses banderilles,
Plein de fureur, il court!
Le cirque est plein de sang!
On se sauve . . . on franchit les grilles!
C'est ton tour maintenant!
Allons! en garde! ah!
Toréador, en garde!
Et songe bien, oui songe en combattant,

Qu'un oeil noir te regarde
Et que l'amour t'attend!

TOUT LE MONDE
Toréador, en garde!

ESCAMILLO
La belle, un mot:
Comment t'appelle-t-on?
Dans mon premier danger
Je veux dire ton nom!

CARMEN
Carmen, Carmencita!
Cela revient au même.

ESCAMILLO
Si l'on te disait que l'on t'aime?

CARMEN
Je répondrais qu'il ne faut pas m'aimer.

ESCAMILLO
Cette réponse n'est pas tendre;
Je me contenterai d'espérer et d'attendre.

CARMEN
Il est permis d'attendre, il est doux d'espérer.

ZUNIGA
Puisque tu ne viens pas Carmen, je reviendrai.

CARMEN
Et vous aurez grand tort.

ZUNIGA
Bah! je me risquerai!

(Sortie d'Escamillo.)

SCÈNE 2

FRASQUITA

Eh! Bien! vite, quelles nouvelles?

LE DANCAIRO

Pas trop mauvaises les nouvelles,
Et nous pouvons encor faire quelques beaux coups!
Mais nous avons besoin de vous.

LES TROIS FEMMES

Besoin de nous!

LE DANCAIRO

Oui, nous avons besoin de vous.

LE DANCAIRO

Nous avons en tête une affaire.

MERCÉDÈS ET FRASQUITA

Est-elle bonne, dites-nous?

LE DANCAIRO

Elle est admirable, ma chère;
Mais nous avons besoin de vous.

LES TROIS FEMMES

De nous?

LES DEUX HOMMES

De vous, car nous l'avouons humblement
Et très respectueusement,
Quand il s'agit de tromperie,
De duperie, de volerie,
Il est toujours bon, sur ma foi,
D'avoir les femmes avec soi,
Et sans elles,
Mes toutes belles,
On ne fait jamais rien de bien.

LES TROIS FEMMES
Quoi! sans nous jamais rien
De bien

LES DEUX HOMMES
N'êtes-vous pas de cet avis?

LES TROIS FEMMES
Si fait, je suis de cet avis.

TOUS LES CINQ
Quand il s'agit de tromperie,
De duperie, de volerie,
Il est toujours bon, sur ma foi,
D'avoir les femmes avec soi,
Et sans elles,
Les toutes belles,
On ne fait jamais rien de bien.

LE DANCAIRO
C'est dit alors, vous partirez.

MERCÉDÈS ET FRASQUITA
Quand vous voudrez.

LE DANCAIRO
Mais tout de suite.

CARMEN
Ah! permettez.
(à Mercédès et à Frasquita)
S'il vous plaît de partir, partez,
Mais je ne suis pas du voyage,
Je ne pars pas, je ne pars pas!

LE REMENDADO
Carmen, mon amour, tu viendras,
Et tu n'auras pas le courage
De nous laisser dans l'embarras.

CARMEN

Je ne pars pas, je ne pars pas.

LE DANCAIRO

Mais au moins la raison, Carmen, tu la diras?

CARMEN

Je la dirai certainement;

**LES DEUX HOMMES AVEC
MERCÉDÈS ET FRASQUITA**

Voyons! Voyons!

CARMEN

La raison, c'est qu'en ce moment.

**LES DEUX HOMMES AVEC
MERCÉDÈS ET FRASQUITA**

Eh bien? Eh bien?

CARMEN

Je suis amoureuse.

LES DEUX HOMMES *(stupéfaits)*

Qu'a-t-elle dit?

LES DEUX FEMMES

Elle dit qu'elle est amoureuse.

LES DEUX HOMMES

Amoureuse!

LES DEUX FEMMES

Amoureuse!

CARMEN

Amoureuse!

LE DANCAIRO

Voyons, Carmen, sois sérieuse.

CARMEN

Amoureuse à perdre l'esprit!

LES DEUX HOMMES

La chose certes nous étonne,
Mais ce n'est pas le premier jour
Où vous aurez su, ma mignonne,
Faire marcher de front le devoir et l'amour.

CARMEN

Mes amis, je serais fort aise
De partir avec vous ce soir
Mais cette fois, ne vous déplaise,
Il faudra que l'amour passe avant le devoir.

LE DANCAIRO

Ce n'est pas là ton dernier mot?

CARMEN

Absolument!

LE REMENDADO

Carmen, il faut
Que tu te laisses attendrir.

TOUS LES QUATRE

Il faut venir, Carmen, il faut venir.
Pour notre affaire,
C'est nécessaire,
Car entre nous—

CARMEN

Quant à cela, je l'admets avec vous:

TOUS LES QUATRE

Quand il s'agit de tromperie,
De duperie, de volerie,
Il est toujours bon, sur ma foi,
D'avoir les femmes avec soi,
Et sans elles,
Mes toutes belles,

On ne fait jamais rien de bien.

LE DANCAIRO
Mais qui donc attends tu?

CARMEN
Presque rien, un soldat qui l'autre jour
        pour me rendre service
S'est fait mettre en prison.

LE REMENDADO
Le fait est délicat.

LE DANCAIRO
Il se peut qu'après tout ton soldat réfléchisse.
Es-tu bien sûre qu'il viendra?

DON JOSÉ *(la voix très éloignée)*
Halte-là!
Qui va là?
Dragon d'Alcala!

CARMEN
Ecoutez!

DON JOSÉ
Où t'en vas-tu par là,
Dragon d'Alcala?

CARMEN
Le voilà!

DON JOSÉ
Moi je m'en vais faire,
A mon adversaire,
Mordre la poussière.
S'il en est ainsi,
Passez mon ami,
Affaire d'honneur
Affaire de coeur,

Pour nous tout est là,
Dragon d'Alcala.

FRASQUITA

C'est un beau Dragon!

MERCÉDÈS

Un très beau Dragon!

LE DANCAIRO

Qui serait pour nous un fier compagnon.

LE REMENDADO

Dis-lui de nous suivre.

CARMEN

Il refusera.

LE DANCAIRO

Mais, essaye, au moins.

CARMEN

Soit! on essayera.

DON JOSÉ *(la voix beaucoup plus rapprochée)*
Halte là!
Qui va là!
Dragon d'Alcala!
Où t'en vas-tu par là,
Dragon d'Alcala?
Exact et fidèle,
Je vais où m'appelle
L'amour de ma belle.
S'il en est ainsi,
Passez mon ami.
Affaire d'honneur,
Affaire de coeur,
Pour nous tout est là,
Dragon d'Alcala!

(Le Remendado se sauve et sort. Le Dancairo le poursuit et sort à son tour entraînant Mercédès et Frasquita. Entre Don José.)

SCÈNE 3

CARMEN
Enfin c'est toi.

DON JOSÉ
Carmen!

CARMEN
Et tu sors de prison?

DON JOSÉ
J'y suis resté deux mois.

CARMEN
Tu t'en plains!

DON JOSÉ
Ma foi non!
Et si c'était pour toi, j'y voudrais être encore.

CARMEN
Tu m'aimes donc?

DON JOSÉ
Je t'adore!

CARMEN
Vos officiers sont venus tout à l'heure,
Ils nous ont fait danser.

DON JOSÉ
Comment? Toi?

CARMEN
Que je meure si tu n'es pas jaloux!

DON JOSÉ

Eh oui, je suis jaloux.

CARMEN

Tout doux, Monsieur, tout doux.

CARMEN

Je vais danser en votre honneur,
Et vous verrez, Seigneur,
Comment je sais moi-même accompagner
    ma danse.
Mettez-vous là, Don José, je commence.

(Elle fait asseoir Don José dans un coin du théâtre. Petite danse, Carmen, du bout des lèvres, fredonne un air qu' elle accompagne avec ses castagnettes. On entend au loin des clairons qui sonnent la retraite. Don José s'approche de Carmen, et l'oblige à arrêter.)

DON JOSÉ

Attends un peu, Carmen, rien qu'un moment,
    arrête.

CARMEN

Et pourquoi, s'il te plaît?

DON JOSÉ

Il me semble, là-bas . . .
Oui, ce sont nos clairons qui sonnent la retraite.
Ne les entends-tu-pas?

CARMEN

Bravo! j'avais beau faire . . . Il est mélancolique
De danser sans orchestre. Et vive la musique
Qui nous tombe du ciel!

(Elle reprend sa chanson. La retraite approche . . . approche . . . approche, passe sous les fenêtres de l'auberge . . . puis s'éloigne. Nouvel effort de Don José pour s'arracher à cette contemplation de Carmen.)

DON JOSÉ

Tu ne m'as pas compris. Carmen, c'est la retraite.
Il faut que, moi, je rentre au quartier pour l'appel.

CARMEN *(stupéfaite)*

Au quartier! pour l'appel! j'étais vraiment trop bête!
Je me mettais en quatre et je faisais des frais
Pour amuser monsieur! Je chantais—
Je dansais.
Je crois, Dieu me pardonne,
Qu'un peu plus, je l'aimais.
Tara tara, c'est le clairon qui sonne!
Il part! il est parti!
Va-t'en donc, canari.
Prends ton shako, ton sabre, ta giberne.
Et va-t'en, mon garçon, retourne à ta caserne.

DON JOSÉ

C'est mal à toi, Carmen, de te moquer de moi;
Je souffre de partir . . . car jamais femme,
Jamais femme avant toi
Aussi profondément n'avait troublé mon âme.

CARMEN

Tara ta ta, mon Dieu . . . c'est la retraite,
Je vais être en retard. Il court, il perd la tête,
Et voilà son amour.

DON JOSÉ

Ainsi tu ne crois pas
A mon amour?

CARMEN

Mais non!

DON JOSÉ

Eh bien! tu m'entendras.

CARMEN

Je ne veux rien entrendre.

DON JOSÉ
Eh bien! tu m'entendras.

CARMEN
Tu vas te faire attendre.

DON JOSÉ *(violemment)*
Tu m'entendras, Carmen, tu m'entendras!

(Il va chercher sous sa veste d'uniforme la fleur de cassie que Carmen lui a jetée. Il montre cette fleur à Carmen.)

DON JOSÉ
La fleur que tu m'avais jetée,
Dans ma prison m'était restée.
Flétrie et sèche, cette fleur
Gardait toujours sa douce odeur
Et pendant des heures entières,
Sur mes yeux fermant mes paupières,
De cette odeur je m'enivrais
Et dans la nuit je te voyais!
Je me prenais à te maudire,
A te détester, à me dire:
Pourquoi faut-il que le destin
L'ait mise là sur mon chemin?
Puis je m'accusais de blasphème
Et je ne sentais en moi-même
Qu'un seul désir, un seul espoir,
Te revoir, Carmen, te revoir!
Car tu n'avais eu qu'à paraître,
Qu'à jeter un regard sur moi
Pour t'emparer de tout mon être
Ô ma Carmen!
Et j'étais une chose à toi!
Carmen, je taime!

CARMEN
Non, tu ne m'aimes pas!

DON JOSÉ
Que dis-tu?

CARMEN

Non, tu ne m'aimes pas!
Non! car si tu m'aimais,
Là-bas, là-bas, tu me suivrais.

DON JOSÉ

Carmen!

CARMEN

Oui! Là-bas, là-bas, dans la montagne . . .

DON JOSÉ

Carmen!

CARMEN

. . . là-bas, là-bas tu me suivrais.
Sur ton cheval tu me prendrais,
Et comme un brave à travers la campagne,
En croupe, tu m'emporterais.
Là-bas, là-bas dans la montagne . . .

DON JOSÉ

Carmen!

CARMEN

. . . là-bas, là-bas tu me suivrais.
Tu me suivrais, si tu m'aimais,
Tu n'y dépendrais de personne;
Point d'officier à qui tu doives obéir
Et point de retraite qui sonne
Pour dire à l'amoureux qu'il est temps de partir.
Le ciel ouvert, la vie errante,
Pour pays l'univers; et pour loi, sa volonté,
Et surtout la chose enivrante:
La liberté! la liberté!

DON JOSÉ

Mon Dieu!

CARMEN

Là-bas, là-bas dans la montagne.

DON JOSÉ

Carmen!

CARMEN

Là-bas, là-bas si tu m'aimais.

DON JOSÉ

Tais toi!

CARMEN

Là-bas, là-bas, tu me suivrais!
Sur ton cheval tu me prendrais!

DON JOSÉ

Ah! Carmen, hélas, tais-toi.
Tais-toi, mon Dieu!

CARMEN

Sur ton cheval tu me prendrais
Et comme un brave
à travers la campagne
Oui tu m'emporterais
Si tu m'aimais.

DON JOSÉ

Hélas! hélas! pitié, Carmen, pitié! Ô mon Dieu!
    hélas!

CARMEN

Oui, n'est-ce pas,
Là-bas, là-bas tu me suivras, tu me suivras!
Là-bas, là-bas tu me suivras,
Tu m'aimes et tu me suivras, là-bas,
Là-bas, emporte-moi!

DON JOSÉ

Ah! tais-toi! tais-toi!
Non, je ne veux plus t'écouter.
Quitter mon drapeau, déserter.
C'est la honte, c'est l'infamie!
Je n'en veux pas!

CARMEN
Eh bien, pars!

DON JOSÉ
Carmen, je t'en prie.

CARMEN
Je ne t'aime plus, je te hais!

DON JOSÉ
Carmen!

CARMEN
Adieu! mais adieu pour jamais!

DON JOSÉ
Eh bien, soit . . . adieu pour jamais!

(Il va en courant jusqu'à la porte. Au moment où il y arrive, on frappe. José s'arrête. Silence. On frappe encore.)

SCÈNE 4

ZUNIGA *(au dehors)*
Holà Carmen!
Holà! Holà!

DON JOSÉ
Qui frappe? qui vient là?

CARMEN
Tais-toi!

ZUNIGA *(faisant sauter la porte)*
J'ouvre moi-même et j'entre.
(Il entre et voit Don José—à Carmen.)
Ah! fi, la belle,
Le choix n'est pas heureux; c'est se mésallier,

De prendre le soldat quand on a l'officier.
Allons! décampe.

(à Don José)

DON JOSÉ

Non.

ZUNIGA

Si fait, tu partiras!

DON JOSÉ

Je ne partirai pas!

ZUNIGA *(le frappant)*

Drôle!

DON JOSÉ *(sautant sur son sabre)*

Tonnerre! il va pleuvoir des coups!

CARMEN *(se jetant entre eux deux)*

Au diable le jaloux!
A moi! à moi!

(Le Dancairo, le Remendado et les Bohémiens paraissent de tous les côtés. Carmen d'un geste montre Zuniga aux Bohémiens. Le Dancairo et le Remendado se jettent sur lui, le désarment.)

CARMEN

Mon officier, l'amour
Vous joue en ce moment un assez vilain tour,
Vous arrivez fort mal et nous sommes forcés,
Ne voulant être dénoncés,
De vous garder au moins pendant une heure.

LE DANCAIRO ET LE REMENDADO

Nous allons, s'il vous plait,
Quitter cette demeure,
Vous viendrez avec nous

124   *Carmen*

CARMEN
C'est une promenade;
Consentez-vous?

LE DANCAIRO ET LE REMENDADO *(le pistolet à la main)*
Répondez, camarade,
Consentez-vous?

LE LIEUTENANT
Certainement,
D'autant plus que votre argument
Est un de ceux auxquels on ne résiste guère
Mais gare à vous plus tard!

LE DANCAIRO *(avec philosophie)*
La guerre, c'est la guerre!
En attendant, mon officier,
Passez devant sans vous faire prier.

CHOEUR
Passez devant sans vous faire prier.

(L'officier sort, emmené par quatre Bohémiens, le pistolet à la main.)

CARMEN *(à Don José)*
Es-tu des nôtres maintenant?

DON JOSÉ
Il le faut bien.

CARMEN
Le mot n'est pas galant,
Mais qu'importe, tu t'y feras
Quand tu verras
Comme c'est beau la vie errante
Pour pays l'univers, pour loi sa volonté,
Et surtout la chose enivrante:
La liberté! la liberté!

TOUS

Le ciel ouvert! la vie errante,
Pour pays l'univers, pour loi sa volonté,
Et surtout la chose enivrante,
La liberté! la liberté!

ACTE TROISIEME

SCÈNE 1

Le rideau se lève sur des rochers . . . site pittoresque et sauvage . . .
Solitude complète et nuit noire. Prélude musical. Un contre-
bandier parait au haut des rochers, puis un autre, puis deux
autres, puis vingt autres çà et là, descendant et escaladant les
rochers. Des hommes portent de gros ballots sur les épaules.

CHOEUR

Ecoute, compagnon, écoute,
La fortune est là-bas, là-bas,
Mais prends garde pendant la route,
Prends garde de faire un faux pas.

LE DANCAIRO, DON JOSÉ, CARMEN, MERCÉDÈS, FRASQUITA

Notre métier est bon, mais pour le faire il faut
Avoir une âme forte,
Le péril est en bas, le péril est en haut,
Il est partout, qu'importe?
Nous allons devant nous, sans souci du torrent,
Sans souci de l'orage,
Sans souci du soldat qui là-bas nous attend,
Et nous guette au passage.
Ecoute, compagnon, écoute, etc.

LE DANCAIRO

Reposons nous une heure ici mes camarades;
Nous, nous allons nous assurer
Si le chemin est libre,
Et que sans algarades
La contrebande peut passer.

CARMEN (*à Don José)*

Que regardes-tu donc?

DON JOSÉ

Je me dis que là-bas
Il existe une bonne et brave vieille
Femme qui me croit honnête homme
Elle se trompe, hélas!

CARMEN

Qui donc est cette femme?

DON JOSÉ

Ah! Carmen sur mon âme, ne raille pas—
Car c'est ma mère.

CARMEN

Eh bien! va la retrouver tout de suite!
Notre métier vois-tu, ne te vaut rien.
Et tu ferais fort bien de partir au plus vite.

DON JOSÉ

Partir, nous séparer?

CARMEN

Sans doute.

DON JOSÉ

Nous séparer, Carmen?
Ecoute si tu redis ce mot—

CARMEN

Tu me tuerais peut-être?

Tu ne réponds rien—
Que m'importe? Après tout, le destin est le maître.

S C È N E 2

*Elle tourne le dos à José et va s'asseoir près de Mercédès et de
Frasquita. Après un instant d'indécision, José s'éloigne à son tour
et va s'étendre sur les rochers. Pendant les dernières réliques de la
scène, Mercédès et Frasquita ont etalé des cartes devant elles.*

FRASQUITA ET MERCÉDÈS
Mêlons!
Coupons!
C'est bien cela.
Trois cartes ici.
Quatre là.

Et maintenant, parlez, mes belles,
De l'avenir donnez-nous des nouvelles;
Dites-nous qui nous trahira,
Dites-nous qui nous aimera.

FRASQUITA
Moi, je vois un jeune amoureux
Qui m'aime on ne peut davantage.

MERCÉDÈS
Le mien est très riche et très vieux,
Mais il parle de mariage.

FRASQUITA
Il me campe sur son cheval
Et dans la montagne il m'entraîne.

MERCÉDÈS
Dans un château presque royal
Le mien m'installe en souveraine.

FRASQUITA
De l'amour à n'en plus finir,
Tous les jours de nouvelles folies.

MERCÉDÈS
De l'or tant que j'en puis tenir,
Des diamants, des pierreries.

FRASQUITA
Le mien devient un chef fameux,
Cent hommes marchent à sa suite.

MERCÉDÈS
Le mien, en croirai-je mes yeux
Il meurt, je suis veuve et j'hérite!

REPRISE DE L'ENSEMBLE
Parlez encor, parlez, mes belles,
De l'avenir donnez-nous des nouvelles.
Dites-nous qui nous trahira,
Dites-nous qui nous aimera.

(Elles recommencent à consulter les cartes.)

FRASQUITA
Fortune!

MERCÉDÈS
Amour!

(Carmen, depuis le commencement de la scène, suivat du regard de jeu de Mercédès et de Frasquita.)

CARMEN
Voyons, que j'essaie à mon tour.
(Elle se met à tourner les cartes.)
Carreau, pique . . . la mort!
J'ai bien lu . . . moi d'abord.
Ensuite lui . . . pour tous les deux la mort.
(A voix basse, tout en continuant à mêler les cartes)
En vain pour éviter les réponses amères,

En vain tu mêleras,
Cela ne sert à rien, les cartes sont sincères
Et ne mentiront pas!
Dans le livre d'en haut si ta page est heureuse,
Mêle et coupe sans peur,
La carte sous tes doigts se tournera joyeuse,
T'annonçant le bonheur.
Mais si tu dois mourir, si le mot redoutable
Est écrit par le sort,
Recommence vingt fois—la carte impitoyable
Répètera: la mort!
Encor! Toujours la mort.

FRASQUITA ET MERCÉDÈS
Parlez encor, parlez, mes belles,
De l'avenir donnez-nous des nouvelles.

CARMEN
Encor!

FRASQUITA
Dites-nous qui nous trahira!

MERCÉDÈS
Dites-nous qui nous trahira!

CARMEN
Encor!

FRASQUITA
Dites-nous qui nous aimera!

MERCÉDÈS
Dites-nous qui nous aimera!

CARMEN
Le désespoir! La mort! la mort!
Encor la mort!

FRASQUITA ET MERCÉDÈS
Parlez encor!

Parlez encor!
Dites-nous qui nous trahira!
Dites-nous qui nous aimera!

MERCÉDÈS

Fortune!

FRASQUITA

Amour!

CARMEN

Toujours la mort!

MERCÉDÈS

Fortune!

FRASQUITA

Amour!

CARMEN

Toujours la mort!

CARMEN, FRASQUITA, MERCÉDÈS

Encor! Encor! Encor!

(Rentrent Dancairo et Remendado.)

SCÈNE 3

CARMEN

Eh bien?

LE DANCAIRO

Eh bien! nous essayerons de passer et nous
        passerons!
Reste là-haut José, garde les marchandises.

FRASQUITA

La route est-elle libre?

LE DANCAIRO

Oui, mais gare aux surprises!
J'ai sur la brèche où nous devons passer
    vu trois douaniers.
Il faut nous en débarrasser.

CARMEN

Prenez les ballots et partons.
Il faut passer, nous passerons.

TOUTES LES TROIS ET LES FEMMES

Quant au douanier, c'est notre affaire,
Tout comme un autre il aime à plaire,
Il aime à faire le galant,
Laissez-nous passer en avant.
Le douanier sera clément.
Le douanier sera charmant.

CARMEN, MERCÉDÈS, FRASQUITA

Il ne s'agit plus de bataille,
Non, il s'agit tout simplement
De se laisser prendre la taille
Et d'écouter un compliment.
S'il faut aller jusqu'au sourire,
Que voulez-vous? on sourira.

TOUTES LES FEMMES

Et d'avance, je puis le dire,
La contrebande passera.

FRASQUITA

En avant!

MERCÉDÈS

En avant!

FRASQUITA

Marchez!

(Tout le monde sort. José ferme la marche et sort en examinant
l'amorce de sa carabine; il sort. Entre Michaela.)

S C È N E 4

MICAELA *(regardant autour d'elle)*
C'est des contrebandiers le refuge
ordinaire. Il est ici, je le verrai.
Et le devoir que m'imposa sa mère,
sans trembler je l'accomplirai.

I

Je dis que rien ne m'épouvante,
Je dis que je réponds de moi,
Mais j'ai beau faire la vaillante,
Au fond du coeur, je meurs d'effroi!
Toute seule en ce lieu sauvage
J'ai peur, mais j'ai tort d'avoir peur;
Vous me donnerez du courage,
Vous me protégerez, Seigneur,
Protégez-moi, protégez-moi, Seigneur.
Je vais voir de près cette femme
Dont les artifices maudits
Ont fini par faire un infâme
De celui que j'aimais jadis;
Elle est dangereuse, elle est belle,
Mais je ne veux pas avoir peur,
Je parlerai haut devant elle,
Vous me protégerez, Seigneur.
Protégez-moi, protégez-moi, Seigneur.

Je ne me trompe pas . . . c'est lui sur ce rocher.
    (appelant) A moi José,
José! Je ne puis approcher. *(avec terreur)*
Mais que fait-il? Il ajuste . . . il fait feu . . .
(On entend un coup de feu.) J'ai trop présumé de
    mes forces, mon Dieu!

*(Elle disparait derrière les rochers. Au même moment entre Escamillo
tenant son chapeau à la main.)*

ESCAMILLO
Quelques lignes plus bas . . .
Et tout était fini.

DON JOSÉ *(son manteau à la main)*
Votre nom, répondez!

ESCAMILLO *(très calme)*
Eh, doucement, l'ami!
Je suis Escamillo, Toréro de Grenade!

DON JOSÉ
Escamillo!

ESCAMILLO
C'est moi.

DON JOSÉ *(remettant son couteau à sa ceinture)*
Je connais votre nom,
Soyez le bienvenu; mais vraiment, camarade,
Vous pouviez y rester.

ESCAMILLO
Je ne vous dis pas non,
Mais je suis amoureux, mon cher, à la folie,
Et celui-là serait un pauvre compagnon,
Qui, pour voit ses amours, ne risquerait sa vie.

DON JOSÉ
Celle que vous aimez est ici?

ESCAMILLO
Justement.
C'est une zingara, mon cher.

DON JOSÉ
Elle s'appelle?

ESCAMILLO

Carmen.

DON JOSÉ

Carmen!

ESCAMILLO

Elle avait pour amant
Un soldat qui jadis a deserté pour elle.
Ils s'adoraient, mais c'est fini, je crois.
Les amours de Carmen ne durent pas six mois.

DON JOSÉ

Vous l'aimez cependant . . .

ESCAMILLO

Je l'aime à la folie!

DON JOSÉ

Mais pour nous enlever nos filles de Bohême,
    savez-vous bien qu'il faut payer?

ESCAMILLO

Soit! on paiera.

DON JOSÉ

Et que le prix se paie à coups de navaja!

ESCAMILLO

A coups de navaja!

DON JOSÉ

Comprenez-vous?

ESCAMILLO

Le discours est très net.
Ce déserteur, ce beau soldat qu'elle aime,
Ou du moins qu'elle aimait.
C'est donc vous?

DON JOSÉ

Oui, c'est moi.

ESCAMILLO

J'en suis ravi, mon cher, et le tour est complet!

DON JOSÉ

Enfin ma colère trouve à qui parler!
Le sang, je l'espère, va bientôt couler.

ESCAMILLO

Quelle maladresse j'en rirais vraiment!
Chercher la maîtresse et trouver l'amant!

ENSEMBLE

Mettez-vous en garde,
Et veillez sur vous!
Tant pis pour qui tarde
A parer les coups!

(Après le dernier ensemble, reprise du combat. Le Toréro glisse et tombe. Entrent Carmen et le Dancairo. Carmen arrête le bras de Don José. Le Toréro se relève; le Remendado, Mercédès, Frasquita et les contrebandiers rentrent pendant ce temps.)

CARMEN

Holà, José!

ESCAMILLO *(se relevant)*

Vrai, j'ai l'âme ravie
Que ce soit vous, Carmen, qui me sauviez la vie.
Quant à toi, beau soldat,
Nous sommes manche à manche, et nous jouerons
la belle,
Le jour où tu voudras reprendre le combat.

LE DANCAIRO

C'est bon, plus de querelle,
Nous, nous allons partir.
(au Toréro)
Et toi, l'ami, bonsoir!

ESCAMILLO

Souffrez au moins qu'avant de vous dire au revoir,
Je vous invite tous aux courses de Séville.
Je compte pour ma part y briller de mon mieux,
Et qui m'aime y viendra.

(à Don José qui fait un geste de menace)

L'ami, tiens toi tranquille. J'ai tout dit.

(à Carmen)

Oui, j'ai tout dit et je n'ai plus ici qu'à faire
mes adieux.

(Jeu de scène. Don José veut s'élancer sur le Toréro. Le Dancairo et Remendado le retiennent. Le Toréro sort très lentement.)

DON JOSÉ *(à Carmen)*

Prends garde à toi, Carmen . . .
je suis las de souffrir.

(Carmen lui répond par un léger haussement d'épaules et s'eloigne de lui.)

LE DANCAIRO

En route, en route, il faut partir.

TOUS

En route, en route, il faut partir.

LE REMENDADO

Halte! Quelqu'un est là qui cherche
à se cacher. *(Il amène Micaela.)*

CARMEN

Une femme!

LE DANCAIRO

Pardieu, la surprise est heureuse!

DON JOSÉ *(reconnaissant Micaela)*

Micaela!

MICAELA

Don José!

DON JOSÉ

Malheureuse!
Que viens-tu faire ici?

MICAELA

Moi, je viens te chercher.
Là-bas est la chaumière
Où sans cesse priant,
Une mère, ta mère,
Pleure hélas sur son enfant.
Elle pleure et t'appelle,
Elle te tend les bras;
Tu prendras pitié d'elle,
José, tu me suivras, tu me suivras!

CARMEN

Va-t'en! va-t'en! Tu feras bien,
Notre métier ne te vaut rien!

DON JOSÉ *(à Carmen)*

Tu me dis de la suivre?

CARMEN

Oui, tu devrais partir.

DON JOSÉ

Pour que toi tu puisses courir
Après ton nouvel amant!
Dût-il m'en coûter la vie,
Non, Carmen je ne partirai pas,
Et la chaîne qui nous lie
Nous liera jusqu'au trépas.

MICAELA *(à Don José)*

Ecoute-moi je t'en prie,
Ta mère te tend les bras,
Cette chaîne qui te lie,
José, tu la briseras.

CHOEUR

Il t'en coutéra la vie!
José, si tu ne pars pas,
Et la chaîne qui vous lie
Se rompra par ton trépas.

DON JOSÉ *(à Micaela)*

Laisse moi!

MICAELA

José!

DON JOSÉ

Car je suis condamné!

CHOEUR

Prends garde, Don José!

DON JOSÉ *(à Carmen)*

Ah! je te tiens, fille damnée,
Et je te forcerai bien
A subir la destinée
Qui rive ton sort au mien!
Dût-il m'en coûter la vie,
Non je ne partirai pas!

CHOEUR

Prends garde! Prends garde, Don José!

MICAELA

Une parole encor, ce sera la dernière!
Hélas! José, ta mère se meurt—et ta mère
Ne voudrait pas mourir sans t'avoir pardonné.

DON JOSÉ

Ma mère se meurt?

MICAELA

Oui, Don José.

DON JOSÉ
Partons, ah, partons!
(à Carmen)
Sois contente je pars, mais nous nous reverrons!

(Il entraine Micaela. On entend le Toréro.)

ESCAMILLO *(au loin)*
Toréador, en garde!
Toréador! Toréador!
Et songe bien, oui,
Songe en combattant,
Qu'un oeil noir te regarde
Et que l'amour t'attend, Toréador,
L'amour t'attend!

(Carmen écoute et se penche sur les rochers. Les Bohémiens chargent leurs ballots et se mettent en marche.)

ACTE QUATRIEME

SCÈNE 1

Une place à Seville. Au fond du théâtre les murailles de la vieille arène. L'entrée du cirque est fermée par un long velum. C'est le jour d'un combat de taureaux. Grand mouvement sur la place. Marchands d'eau, d'oranges, d'éventails, etc.

CHOEUR
A deux cuartos,
Des éventails pour s'éventer,
Des oranges pour grignotter.
Le programme avec les détails,
Du vin! De l'eau!

Des cigarettes!
A deux cuartos,
Le programme avec les détails
Du vin! De l'eau!
Des cigarettes!
Señoras et caballeros . . .

(Pendant ce premier choeur sont entrés les deux officiers du deuxième Acte ayant au bras les deux Bohémiennes, Mercédès et Frasquita.)

ZUNIGA
Des oranges, vite.

PLUSIEURS MARCHANDS *(se précipitant)*
En voici.
Prenez, prenez, mesdemoiselles.

UN MARCHAND *(à l'officier qui paie)*
Merci, mon officier, merci.

LES AUTRES MARCHANDS
Celles-ci, señor, sont plus belles.
A deux cuartos,
A deux cuartos,
Señoras et caballeros.

MARCHAND DE PROGRAMMES
Le programme avec les détails.

AUTRES MARCHANDS
Du vin.

AUTRES MARCHANDS
De l'eau.

AUTRES MARCHANDS
Des cigarettes.

ZUNIGA
Holà! des éventails.

UN BOHÉMIEN *(se précipitant)*
Voulez-vous aussi des lorgnettes!

(On entend de grands cris au dehors, des fanfares, etc. C'est l'ar-
rivée de la Cuadrilla. Entrée des enfants.)

ENFANTS
Les voici, les voici!
Voici la quadrille!

CHOEUR
Oui, les voici!
Voici la quadrille!

ENFANTS ET CHOEUR
Les voici, voici la quadrille,
La Quadrille des Toréros,
Sur les lances le soleil brille
En l'air toques et sombreros
Les voici, voici la quadrille,
La Quadrille des Toréros.

(Defilé de la quadrille. Pendant ce defilé, le choeur chante le
morceau suivant. Entrée des alguazils.)

Voici, débouchant sur la place,
Voici d'abord, marchant au pas,
L'alguazil à vilaine face!
A bas, à bas!
(Entrée des chulos et des banderilleros.)
Et puis saluons au passage,
Saluons les hardis chulos,
Bravo! vivat! gloire au courage!
Voici les hardis chulos.
Voyez les banderilleros!
Voyez quel air de crânerie,
Quels regards et de quel éclat
Etincelle la broderie
De leur costume de combat.
(Entrée des picadors.)
Une autre quadrille s'avance,

Voyez les picadors! comme ils sont beaux!
Comme ils vont du fer de leur lance
Harceler le flanc des taureaux.

(Paraît enfin Escamillo, ayant près de lui Carmen radieuse et dans un costume éclatant.)

L'espada! Escamillo!
C'est l'espada, la fine lame,
Celui qui vient terminer tout,
Qui paraît à la fin du drame
Et qui frappe le dernier coup!
Vive Escamillo, ah bravo!

ESCAMILLO *(à Carmen)*
Si tu m'aimes, Carmen, tu pourras tout à l'heure
    être fière de moi.

CARMEN
Je t'aime, Escamillo, je t'aime et que je meure
Si j'ai jamais aimé quelqu'un autant que toi!

TOUS LES DEUX
Ah, je t'aime!
Oui, je t'aime.

(De la foule se rangeant sur le passage de l'alcade.)

LES ALGUAZILS
Place, place au seigneur alcade!

(Petite marche à l'orchestre. Sur cette marche entre au fond l'alcade précédé et suivi des Alguazils. Pendant ce temps Frasquita et Mercédès s'approchent de Carmen.)

FRASQUITA
Carmen, un bon conseil, ne reste pas ici.

CARMEN
Et pourquoi, s'il te plait?

FRASQUITA

Il est là.

CARMEN

Qui donc?

FRASQUITA

Lui, Don José.
Dans la foule il se cache; regarde.

CARMEN

Oui, je le vois.

FRASQUITA

Prends garde.

CARMEN

Je ne suis pas femme à trembler devant lui, je l'attends—et je vais lui parler.

(L'alcade est entré dans le cirque. La populace suit et la foule en se retirant a dégagé Don José. Carmen reste seule au premier plan.)

SCÈNE 2

CARMEN

C'est toi?

DON JOSÉ

C'est moi.

CARMEN

L'on m'avait avertie
Que tu n'étais pas loin, que tu devais venir,
L'on m'avait même dit de craindre pour ma vie,
Mais je suis brave et n'ai pas voulu fuir.

DON JOSÉ

Je ne menace pas, j'implore, je supplie,
Notre passé, je l'oublie,
Carmen, nous allons tous deux
Commencer une autre vie,
Loin d'ici, sous d'autres cieux.

CARMEN

Tu demandes l'impossible,
Carmen jamais n'a menti,
Son âme reste inflexible.
Entre elle et toi, c'est fini.

DON JOSÉ

Carmen, il en est temps encore,
O ma Carmen, laisse-moi
Te sauver, toi que j'adore,
Et me sauver avec toi!

CARMEN

Non, je sais bien que c'est l'heure,
Je sais bien que tu me tueras.
Mais que je vive ou que je meure,
Non, je ne te céderai pas!

DON JOSÉ

Carmen, il est temps encore,
O ma Carmen, laisse-moi
Te sauver, toi que j'adore,
Et me sauver avec toi.

CARMEN

Pourquoi t'occuper encore
D'un coeur qui n'est plus à toi?
En vain tu dis: je t'adore,
Tu n'obtiendras rien de moi.

DON JOSÉ

Tu ne m'aimes donc plus?
Tu ne m'aimes donc plus?

CARMEN
Non, je ne t'aime plus.

DON JOSÉ
Mais moi, Carmen, je t'aime encore;
Carmen, Carmen, moi je t'adore!

CARMEN
A quoi bon tout cela? que de mots superflus!

DON JOSÉ
Eh bien, s'il le faut, pour te plaire,
Je resterai bandit, tout ce que tu voudras.
Tout, tu m'entends, mais ne me quitte pas,
    ah ma Carmen,
Ah, souviens-toi du passé, nous nous aimions
    naguère!
Ah, ne me quitte pas, Carmen, ne me quitte pas!

CARMEN
Jamais Carmen ne cédera,
Libre elle est née et libre elle mourra!

CHOEUR *(dans le cirque)*
Viva! la course est belle,
Sur le sable sanglant
Le taureau qu'on harcèle
S'élance en bondissant.
Viva! bravo! victoire,
Frappé juste en plein coeur,
Voyez, voyez!
Victoire!

(Pendant ce choeur, silence de Carmen et de Don José. Tous deux écoutent. En entendant les cris de: "Victoire," Carmen à laissé échapper un "Ah!" d'orgueil et de joie. Don José ne perd pas Carmen de vue. Le choeur terminé, Carmen fait un pas du côté du cirque.)

DON JOSÉ *(se plaçant devant elle)*
Où vas-tu?

CARMEN

Laisse-moi!

DON JOSÉ

Cet homme qu'on acclame,
C'est ton nouvel amant!

CARMEN *(voulant passer)*

Laisse-moi!

DON JOSÉ

Sur mon âme,
Carmen, tu ne passeras pas,
Carmen, c'est moi que tu suivras!

CARMEN

Laisse-moi, Don José! Je ne te suivrai pas.

DON JOSÉ

Tu vas le retrouver, dis . . . tu l'aimes donc?

CARMEN

Je l'aime,
Je l'aime, et devant la mort même,
Je répéterai que je l'aime!

(Fanfares et reprise du choeur dans le cirque.)

DON JOSÉ

Ainsi, le salut de mon âme,
Je l'aurai perdu pour que toi,
Pour que tu t'en ailles, infâme!
Entre ses bras, rire de moi.
Non, par le sang, tu n'iras pas,
Carmen, c'est moi que tu suivras!

CARMEN

Non! non! jamais!

DON JOSÉ

Je suis las de te menacer.

CARMEN

Eh bien! frappe-moi donc ou laisse-moi passer.

CHOEUR

Victoire!

DON JOSÉ

Pour la dernière fois, démon,
Veux-tu me suivre?

CARMEN

Non! non!
Cette bague autrefois tu me l'avais donnée,
Tiens!

(Elle la jette à la volée.)

DON JOSÉ *(le poignard à la main, s'avançant sur Carmen)*
Eh bien, damnée!

(Carmen recule. Don José la poursuit. Pendant ce temps fanfares dans le cirque.)

CHOEUR

Toréador, en garde,
Toréador! Toréador!
Et songe bien, oui, en combattant
Qu'un oeil noir te regarde
Et que l'amour t'attend, Toréador,
L'amour t'attend!

(José a frappé Carmen. Elle tombe morte. Le velum s'ouvre. On sort du cirque.)

DON JOSÉ

Vous pouvez m'arrêter. C'est moi qui l'ai tuée!

(Escamillo paraît sur les marches du cirque. José se jette sur le corps de Carmen.)

Ah Carmen! Ma Carmen adorée!

ABOUT THE TRANSLATOR

SONYA FRIEDMAN is the innovator and writer of subtitles for opera on television (*The Metropolitan Opera Presents* and *Live From Lincoln Center*) and the creator of supertitles for live opera performances. Her translations are currently used by opera companies throughout the U.S. and Canada. Ms. Friedman has translated over 100 operas; *Carmen* remains one of her favorites.

ABOUT THE ILLUSTRATOR

RENÉ BULL (1872–1942), born in Dublin, Ireland, gained his reputation on a news magazine as one of England's most talented and prolific artists. Greatly influenced by Asian art, Bull went on to a celebrated career illustrating children's books and is especially admired for his editions of *Fables de la Fontaine, Uncle Remus, The Arabian Nights,* and *The Rubáiyát of Omar Khayyam.*